A Month of Somedays

A Month of Somedays

How One Woman
Made the Most of Now

Catherine Cleary

LONDUBH BOOKS

First published in 2012
by Londubh Books
18 Casimir Avenue, Harold's Cross, Dublin 6w, Ireland
www.londubh.ie
1 3 5 4 2
Origination by Londubh Books; cover by siné design
Printed by ScandBook AB, Falun, Sweden
ISBN: 978-1-907535-28-4

For Maria Ruane (1967-2011) who wasn't given enough days

Contents

Acknowledgements

Thanks to Liam for his love and support. And to Shane, Peter and Isaac for their enthusiasm for all the crazy things their mother did.

Thanks to:

Marie Comiskey for her patience and sense of humour; my fellow allotmenters and Dublin City Council assistant area manager Bruce Phillips for all the work at Weaver Court Allotments; Anne Leonard and all the wonderful teachers at her Bikram studio; Deng Xiao e or Grace Mullins as I know her for her fascinating lessons; Dr Ronan Murphy and the sports scientists at Dublin City University's School of Health and Human Performance, whose expertise and time were hugely helpful; Professor Shane O'Meara, head of the Department of Neuroscience at Trinity College Dublin, for his insights into learning; nutrition expert Susan Jane White and restaurateur Ronan Ryan for help with a project that might have been; Domini and Peaches Kemp and the staff at Itsa Bagel headquarters for their generosity and time; great friends Alison, Roisin, Carol, Paul, Pauline and Mick for their interest and feedback; the book club crew who kept me thinking about the reader: Anne, Andy, Avril, Eimear, Ger, Tara and Yvonne; Trish and Seb for happy days in magical Les Monts; my parents Joan and Shane and in laws Benny and Catherine for encouragement and babysitting; Christine and Nimo for keeping three boys very happy while I worked.

And a huge thanks to Mark, Sean, Catherine and Maeve for allowing me to write about their beloved Maria.

Foreword

It's September 2012 and I'm looking down the wrong end of the telescope at last year's me. September is my January, the month when I think about new beginnings, a throwback to the days of new pencil cases and stiff school shoes. It's been a life changing time in one way but I am beginning to realise that every year is life changing. From the moment we're born we change. We grow up, we grow out, we grow grey, we grow old.

I suppose when we talk about the life changing things we mean the big things: those events that rip us from one set of circumstances and throw us into another: the births, deaths and marriages, not the daily stuff, the everyday routine. But for me it's been a year of changing everyday life.

My days are different now from how they were just over a year ago, thanks to some of the things I did these past months. Every day I pick up a flute and play some music. Most of the time no one is listening other than the dog, who puts her nose in the air and howls. At some point in the day I wonder how the weeds are doing in the allotment and feel a twinge of responsibility to go and water or harvest or weed a plot of inner city soil. It's been a tough season for gardeners. This summer my patch became a playground for fox cubs, a feeding ground for killer slugs and a place where tender seedlings found it just too cold to survive.

Most days, at the point when I feel overwhelmed by life, I grab a couple of towels and go and sweat in a room full of similarly sweating people or pull on minimalist running shoes and run away up the road as fast as my aching legs will carry me.

It's been a year in which time and place seemed to come together and make sense. I ran in the rain and the cold and found them refreshing (most of the time). I smelled the seasons shift before they were fully in place: new grass, the first puff of smoke from open fires, the smell of things beginning to grow or starting to die.

In warm sunshine this June bank holiday I ran the 10k Women's Mini Marathon in (just) under an hour, wearing funny shoes with separated toes. I took these off for the last few hundred metres and ran barefoot up the cool smooth whiteness of the bus lane markings on Leeson Street. I felt the sadness at the heart of this event: the number of women running and walking with ghosts at their heels, still putting one foot in front of the other despite life crushing losses.

I reached for my schoolgirl French and found it still there, rusty and under used but so much easier than the Mandarin I tried to hammer into my head. I attempted to curb my Internet compulsion and began to realise the meditative value of plain old work. And just recently I started bird watching, snatched moments of it, after moving my desk to a big window. Now I can see gulls, gannets, crows, magpies and pigeons flap and glide against a cloudscape that is never the same from one moment to the next.

Even though life changing things happen to us, I believe we remain the same. Taking a bit of control over everyday life to make small things change has not transformed me into a new person. I am not a natural optimist or extrovert but challenging the habits of the daily grind, taking on an everyday life changing set of challenges, has encouraged me to try on those attributes like an unfamiliar set of clothes. This is not a prescriptive book, a how to manual for personal transformation. It's an account of an attempt, involving lots of flapping and ungainly fluttering and just a few moments of pure blissful gliding.

Introduction

Three thousand six hundred and forty socks and an unpainted skirting board.
This was to be a book that began with defeat and ended with something else, not quite triumph but something better. 'I am defeated,'
I wrote many months ago. The unpainted stretch of dusty skirting
board three years after the builder left our house was defeating me.
The five pairs of socks to be washed, paired and put away were a
daily defeat, coming to an annual sock count of 3640.

My freelance work as a journalist had seeped into every crevice
of my day. The laptop had sidled on to the kitchen counter, along
with a strong compulsion to 'just check an email or send a quick
tweet' while stirring dinner, with a toddler clamped to one leg, in that
tired and hungry hour before my husband walked through the door.
It was a regime that left me frazzled and short tempered.

And there was a wider mood of defeat, so strong you could
almost taste it in the air. At times it seemed the only certainty was
uncertainty. The transformation of Affluent Ireland to Austerity
Ireland had left few people feeling untouched. In an astonishing
reversal of fortune we have been left feeling that there is nothing
solid under our feet. Comfort zones lie blasted to pieces and many
of us have to look at ourselves in new ways, reassessing what is
important and how best to use our time.

The part of me that wasn't a working from home mother of
three dreamt of a day, some day, when I would have time to do
the things I've always wanted to do. I think everyone carries this
someday stuff with them. We take these ideas out and polish them
in moments of reflection, on trains or planes. They lie in wait for
us at the bottom of the second glass of wine, on the last night of a
holiday or in the time before we fall asleep.

Many of the things I longed to do were things I could have done
in my twenties, instead of watching episodes of *Friends* or fretting

about whether the phone was going to ring. But much of that time was taken up with establishing a career, working exciting and stressful hours. In the recession of the 1980s my generation didn't get a gap year, an opportunity to explore aspects of ourselves that did not lead directly to gainful employment. There was rent to be paid.

Most people dream of an escape from the daily grind into something that seems more meaningful or fulfilling: the book they will write when they retire to a wood panelled study that exists somewhere in the future; the neighbourhood bakery they will put into a shuttered and empty premises they pass every day (called Pie in the Sky because it's never going to happen). 'One day, maybe,' we sigh, then close the lid on the dream and put on another pot of pasta for dinner.

Work, money, family and time all separate us from these other ambitions. The biggest barrier is time. As we get older life seems to get busier until it takes a two week holiday to gives us back the sense of owning our own time. Then we breathe better, sleep better, see things more clearly and taste things more strongly. We come back rested and refreshed to the land of 4am anxiety attacks and please give me a minute and never enough time.

My parents used to tell the story of a musician friend who was the mother of small children. She had a large wooden playpen and a busy house. When it came time for her to practise her cello she would clamber into the playpen with the instrument and a chair. She would sit and practise while her children played in the space outside, the music rising from the instrument while around her the chaos and tumble of small children went on.

I didn't have a playpen to climb into but I needed to build boundaries around work and family and play. I wanted to learn again, as I did when I was a child, stretch myself and see what I could do.

And so the idea for this book was born. No one was going to give me a minute, much less sixty or even ninety of them, every day for thirty days. So what if I just gave them to myself, roped off a small chunk of uninterrupted time to try something, kickstart a habit or pursue an idea? Thirty given days, given by me to me, to make something happen. Each one a month of somedays. I had a list of six things I wanted to do: learn to play the flute; an allotment project from scratch; an intensive daily yoga class; take on a fitness challenge; learn Mandarin; and start a small business venture.

Could I somehow fit these things into everyday life; take a gap year without leaving home? I was anchored down in Dublin 8 and would be for the foreseeable future. My heart lay firmly with my family, my husband Liam and our three sons. It was just my head that needed some fresh air. Could I do a gap year from my kitchen table, take a small amount of time out of everyday life to make more of every day? Or would it just pile the pressure on to my already creaking state of mind? The subtitle to this book could just as easily be 'The Midlife Crisis of an Irish Mammy.' In typical mammy martyrdom, instead of Botox or a boyfriend I was going to shoehorn more work into an already busy life.

The male midlife crisis is well documented; the female one has a more muted voice, particularly in Ireland. I see my generation of career focused women trying to construct new selves from the limited options available to us as a large swathe of over mortgaged forty somethings. Many of us came to motherhood later than our mothers did and we're all grappling with the cult of youthfulness: a very particular tyranny of ideas of female beauty and the kidult world we're encouraged to create around ourselves. God help us all when the menopause hits. Right now we're asking: 'There has to be more to it than this, hasn't there?' as panic sets in about the time we may have left.

When you hit forty life can seem like a litany of lasts: the last breastfeed, the last Babygro, the last buggy ride, the last conversation you had with someone who is gone. Life can seem as if it's shutting down, a series of small endings, one small bodily function at a time, especially when you're a woman. You let go of the things that defined you and struggle to find something new.

I wanted to be a beginner at things again, not an ender. I wanted to have lots of firsts in my future, along with the lasts. As an adult beginner I came to things I'd never done before with nothing more than a desire to keep opening new doors in life while acknowledging that others had closed; to keep riding the unsettling waves of change rather than lying down and letting them wash over me.

'You want to step off the edge,' someone said, as I described the idea for the book. 'How long does it take to form a habit?' someone else asked. Another friend burst out laughing and assumed I was going to have sex every day for thirty days.

'You're nuts,' sports scientist Professor Niall Moyna of Dublin City University said bluntly, as I sat in his office explaining this project in the stock self helpish phrases I'd worked up to describe it. 'You need to be taken to Saint Pat's.' At times I thought he was right. I was just bonkers. There was very little wrong with my life, other than a few first world anxieties and the impulse to find something I could call myself again underneath the pile of discarded socks.

As a journalist I had interviewed dozens of people who had done extraordinary things within the limits of ordinary life. What's so ordinary about ordinary life anyway? I wanted to find out what it would do to me to spend chunks of thirty days doing six separate things, activities so outside my routine and comfort zone that they would make my head spin. I wanted to discover whether I could find out anything about myself or the nature of contentment in the process.

What I didn't know when I wrote about defeat was that during my kitchen table gap year life would toss me a breeze block of loss, an event no one in my circle of close friends saw coming. In one way it made everything in these pages seem extravagantly pointless. In another it made them all the more important.

1

Make It Sing

I knew it was going to be difficult. I didn't realise just how embarrassing the first step would feel. I am standing in a front room in a suburban house in south Dublin making what can only be described as a horrible noise. In my dream first flute lesson my new teacher would marvel at the discovery of a natural, a forty one year old prodigy, born to play the flute. But there is no natural ability resonating around this music room, just a strange anti music, a noise that is pleasant only when it stops. As I blow across the hole in the gleaming silver head joint of my hired flute my shoulders are clenched up around my ears and I'm starting to feel a dizzy buzz in my head as my breath runs out.

My teacher, Marie Comiskey, makes a deep honeyed note with her beautiful gold and copper flute that resonates around the room. I make an awful thready whistle with my instrument. My breath seems to be coming from only the top layer of my lungs and emerging in a wispy unfocused flow over the lip plate of the flute. Worst of all I am rigid with self consciousness. After a few minutes I have to roll my shoulders back repeatedly to unkink the knots of tension.

I've always wanted to play the flute and when I picked up my hired instrument a few days earlier I could hardly believe I was going to assemble this intimidatingly beautiful instrument and try to play it. When I told the woman in the music shop my plan over the phone – to learn to play the flute in thirty days – she paused diplomatically and said, 'Well it's not the worst idea I've ever heard.'

Three months rental would cost me €86.25. If I wanted to buy the flute at the end I would pay off the balance of €489.75, bringing the total cost of the instrument to €575. She recommended that I rent a Trevor James Privilege flute. There are cheaper versions but, she explains, this one will be the equivalent of learning to drive in a new car rather than a clapped out banger that takes some coaxing. With that I'm sold.

They've seen lots of adult learners coming to hire flutes in this Dublin instrument shop. 'Ninety per cent of them have stuck with it,' the woman said in that first chat on the phone. 'They're having an absolute ball and they're just sorry they didn't start it sooner.'

I opened the heavy black case when I got home and was struck by the beauty of the instrument. It was packed in three sections, each one gleaming like the best wedding cutlery in its separate purple velvet compartment. I had no idea how to put it together and was too nervous to try until I got to my first lesson.

As well as being a teacher, Marie is a professional flautist, who regularly performs with the National Symphony Orchestra and the RTÉ Concert Orchestra. She studied with Professor Doris Keogh at the Royal Irish Academy of Music and with Edward Beckett (a nephew of Samuel Beckett) in London. I found her great fun. She was tickled at the idea of what I was doing. But as a teacher she wasn't going to let me take any shortcuts.

Now I was beginning to appreciate the challenge. Part of the problem was my cockiness about my ability to breathe. Whatever about mastering the art of producing a sound from the flute, I considered myself a bit of an expert at breathing, with years of yoga and three epidural free childbirth experiences under my belt. But something was badly wrong each time I raised the instrument to my lips and tried to play. It was as if invisible hands were squeezing the air out of the lower parts of my lungs. I was out of breath and gasping for air at the end of the shortest notes.

Towards the end of the first lesson I hit the lowest point when I put my right hand the wrong way round on the lower keys, leaving me with both hands on the same side of the flute like a mediaeval court jester tootling jokily on his instrument. Then Sean, Marie's next student, came in and listened to me make my puffy *pfft* noise as he waited for his lesson to start, running his fingers expertly along the keys for his complicated jazzy beatboxy self composition. He gave a short performance that seemed to be at a level of virtuosity that I could only imagine. 'He's twelve,' I thought. 'I'm mortified.'

I took the flute out at home later that day and it took a while to put it together and position my fingers on the right keys. It all felt alien and difficult, like trying to write with my left hand. It was also surprisingly physical. Although this metre or so of silver plated metal is not a heavy instrument my muscles were tense from holding my arms at a strange angle. My neck clicked painfully.

I looked up *embouchure*, from the French word *bouche* for mouth. It's the positioning of the mouth that you need to learn to play the flute. Effectively you try to blow through the tiniest opening in your mouth without tensing your lips. It's a bit like trying to whistle while blowing a kiss. Your lower lip is pushed out level with the upper one. It's a face you make only if you are playing the flute and the muscles around your lips have to be trained to do it well. I'm picturing that peculiar fish faced look that comes from a bad lip collagen injection every time I try to make it. The classic beginner's mistake is to tense up the face so your mouth is a rigid line and the airstream is wispy and weak. The other error is trying to puff out your cheeks to generate the air. A good *embouchure* is much more relaxed than that. 'Imagine saying the word "pure",' Marie advised. On my bike later, I make an *embouchure* into the wind all the way home. I look like a demented plastic surgery victim.

Without a good *embouchure* the tone of the flute will not be good. The tinier the opening in your mouth, the longer your breath will last, giving the tone depth and ballast. The French flautist, Marcel Moyse, advised 'time, patience and intelligent work' to perfect the *embouchure*. I'm not sure if I have any of these resources at this stage.

The other thing that will affect the tone is the air coming from the two bellows that are my lungs. It's helpful to think of that air in terms of a colour – dark brown or purple air coming from the lower regions of the lung. At the moment I'm breathing wispy yellow puffs from the upper layers. I'm going to have to breathe like an opera singer to get anything other than an unpleasant waspy whine out of the instrument.

'You will feel like throwing this through the window,' Marie warned. 'Not at nearly €600 to replace it,' I think. Two days later I see exactly what she means.

Day Two

I can't practise the flute for ninety minutes a day, everyone from the flute hire shop to my teacher has told me. So I carve it up into six fifteen minute segments. It's a different kind of screen break to stand up from the computer and go to coax a sound out of the instrument.

At first it feels deeply frustrating; then I slowly start to hear a sound I don't hate. It's still far from Marie's deep resonant note but it's got a bit of body to it. As a child I learned to play the piano, starting when I was about thirteen. I had a gifted teacher in the shape of a Dominican nun who loved music and was born to teach. As well as the scale exercises and the dry grade works, she found magical pieces of music to match the ability of her students and draw them out. She was a teacher who taught children how to play music rather than how to pass exams, showing them early on the pleasure that could result from the discipline and hard work of practice.

Unfortunately she was transferred away and I was passed on to a teacher whose style was much more old school. This woman held my hands to the keys with her own claw like nicotine stained hands. I can still remember the feeling of those hard hands with sharp and painted nails, jabbing my fingers on to the correct keys. I gave up the piano about a year later and the ability to play evaporated quickly.

In my twenties I bought a secondhand piano at a furniture auction and had it shifted, at huge expense, into the tiny cottage where I lived. In a flurry of enthusiasm I bought a few books of music, sat and tried to relearn what I had lost. It proved too difficult, so before my next house move I paid someone another fortune to take the piano back to the auction rooms. I notched up the misguided piano purchase to experience.

But now my sight reading is coming back and soon I am able to play '*Au Clair de la Lune*' (a four note baby tune version of this simple French folk song) from the beginner flute book, sounding a bit like music instead of a series of disjointed notes. I worry that I'm charging ahead into pieces instead of trying to hold those long notes and doing my tone exercises. But I'm keen to get to the music.

It strikes me that learning as an adult is difficult in all kinds of ways. My starter flute book is full of pictures of children doing what I'm struggling to learn, with cartoon illustrations designed for young learners. As an adult, being told you are doing something wrong is difficult to hear without feeling stung by it. But those mistakes are the means of learning. By my last session of the day I've added a middle C to my four note repertoire. It wakes the two year old in his bedroom next door. The dog has started to whine when I practise. At this rate I will be banished to the garden where no one can hear me flute.

Day Three

The first practice session of the day is a definite backward step. I can produce a tune but it sounds watery and feeble. Sometimes it feels as if I'm whistling or even humming the notes over the blow hole of the flute rather than producing notes from the instrument. I can suddenly relate to teenage boys whose voices are breaking. There is the same uncertainty as to what sound is going to come out each time I raise the flute to my lips. You might fluff a piano note but at least the instrument will make its sound. With the flute there is none of that certainty: in some practice sessions it starts out terrible and ends worse.

The thready thin sound is back and I run out of breath after three or four notes. I'm getting dizzy playing the few notes in '*Au Clair de la Lune*'. The dog who normally sleeps at my feet in my office as I type has gone in search of peace. I improvise a music stand with boxes on the windowsill. I need to stand in front of a mirror but there's nowhere to balance the music book. At this point I wonder if the world really needs another bad flute player?

And then, like a ray of warm sun, I am stumbling my way through a piece in the beginner book when I suddenly realise I'm playing a piece of music I love. It's Offenbach's 'Barcarolle' from the opera *The Tales of Hoffman*, the gentle swaying melody written to mimic the rolling of a gondola in water. You will hear it starting quietly with just a few instruments, strings and wind, and building until the majesty of a full orchestra pushes it to a grand blowsy finish. This version is just a snippet of the composition, using the limited number of notes I know. But finding I can play it is wonderful. It's like seeing an old friend in a room full of strangers. I still can't keep a consistent note or tone but this is enough to make me go on.

Day Four

The second lesson. Each time I stand in Marie's music room I feel as if the clouds are clearing to reveal that the small hill I started to climb has become a cliff face. I go along just a little smug. Look at me, I can play a tune, albeit breathlessly and shakily and with a dizziness that might be the precursor to a full faint. But a tune. After just three days. Then, stickler that she is, Marie points out that my shoulders are rigid and rising as far as my ears, I'm breathing only from the top of my rib cage (a problem that could take months to get over) and my fingers are not resting over the keys carefully enough to let me play the notes in quick succession.

Part of my problem is the bodily cringe that sets in every time I try to play the flute in front of anyone, that sense of being ridiculously bad that turns me into a hunch shouldered shallow breather. As a child, I presume, I would not have brought any of this kind of baggage to a lesson. And I wouldn't have decades of responding to stress by clenching my shoulders and shallow breathing, which makes playing the flute virtually impossible.

Then the tonguing starts. At this point I go back to square minus one. Tonguing is much less fun than it sounds. It involves making a 'ta' sound with the tip of your tongue on the roof of your mouth to punctuate each note. It has wrecked my *embouchure*. Each time I do it my lips open more than they should and it seems impossible to keep the stream of air narrow and focused. I practise it in the car on the long drive home in torrential rain and I can't stop my lips puffing just fractionally every time I do it. It's rubbing your stomach, patting your head and walking a tightrope all at once.

I realise now why anyone who knows anything about the flute looked at me with polite forbearance when I told them my thirty day goal. They were giving me the same look I might give a pregnant woman who tells me she is going to get through labour with essential oils and visualisation – the 'she has no idea but let's just humour her, nod and smile, nod and smile' kind of look.

The labour pains are kicking in now. And I'm close to throwing in the towel.

Day Five

The dog thinks I'm losing it. I'm lying on the floor with a Harry Potter book on my stomach, taking deep breaths. It's a breathing exercise that I skipped for the first few days because, to my mind, I was the queen of breathing.

Flute breathing is much like a swimmer's breathing. A big fast gulp of air into the lower lungs, then a slow steady, controlled release. There's no slow inhale and slow exhale like yoga, no sucking in the stomach. Your shoulders don't move. Nothing moves above the lower rib cage. When you do it you suddenly get the feeling of your lungs as balloons, with the diaphragm working to inflate the balloons by moving downwards and pushing out the stomach wall. I'm learning how to breathe all over again. Dispiritingly, Marie has told me that learning to breathe well enough to play the flute can take months.

Day Six

It's my cousin's wedding and I've packed the flute and music book in the bottom of my overnight bag. I'm not going to whip it out in the entertainment part of the night, though my family would wildly applaud chutzpah like that. But I do plan to squeeze in a practice session in the hotel where we're staying. I imagine a minor breakthrough. I will find my sound in some anonymous hotel room with no children in the building, at least none that are mine, and none of the toy strewn chaos and clothes horse clutter of home.

It's not to be. We get a late night call from my normally supremely unflappable mother in law. Our eldest is suddenly sick, with a raging temperature, vomiting and groaning. We check out of our room at 1am and drive through dark Longford roads to get home, both of us with thoughts of a late night dash to the nearest hospital. But when we arrive he's fine. The tempest has passed: he's pale and still groaning but mainly sleeping.

Day Seven

A race back to Dublin for what will turn out to be the most frustrating six hours of my summer. I am wearing my best dress, my face painted by a young woman on a Brown Thomas make up counter, heels on, hair brushed. In a rainstorm I'm teetering across a hardcore path to an old storage building on a NAMA site. Inside is the set of *MasterChef Ireland*: I've agreed to be one of fourteen pretend restaurant diners eating the dishes prepared by twelve contestants. In the end I spend hours sitting on a hard plastic chair eating lukewarm or cold food and trying to come up with pithy lines about it to a camera as my mascara drifts further down my face. I begin to feel 'Stockholm Syndrome' set in. As the hours go on I realise that if I make the cut my words of wisdom will get a couple of minutes of airtime and I will sound mean and churlish about an undercooked piece of hake that some poor individual has shed tears over in the kitchen. No flute today and I miss it. Just exhaustion and defeat.

Day Eight

Another lesson and Marie is wondering if she's been too hard on me. But she knows how tight the deadline is and she's rushing me through, like a mountain guide who realises that we're not going to make camp at nightfall at this rate. I'm enjoying the lessons more now. I've stopped taking corrections personally, as if they're a slight.

She adjusts the way I'm holding the flute and it suddenly feels more natural and relaxed. My fingers aren't stiffening over the keys in the same way and it's easier to hold them curled and close to the smooth silver caps, giving me a better chance of making notes in time. She laughs, claps her hands in triumph and tells me, 'Now you look like a flute player.' I'm thankful for my rudimentary ability to read music, which makes a semblance of a tune out of things I try.

I still have a lot to learn about basic musicianship. The concentration needed to read the notes, get the rhythm and try to remember where the notes are on the instrument is intensely challenging.

My eldest son is practising his violin and asks me to duet with him. His school has started a music project involving three class groups learning either recorder or violin. I'm nervous that nothing will come out of my flute in the way of sound but we both slowly go through one of his very simple songs, playing in time and in tune. He's thrilled and I'm blown away with pleasure of it, making music with my baby boy. The four year old tries to join in with his drum. If I achieve nothing else this has felt like a big moment.

It's almost 11pm before I get a chance to get near the flute. Marie has set me some serious homework and I'm stretching my five note repertoire beyond the point where my brain has caught up. I go back to play 'The Prince of Denmark' and find the low D disappearing in a waspy prickly wheeze. Tomorrow I'm drawing a series of circles to give myself the fingering chart for going up and down the scales, then I'm buying a music stand. The trouser stand I'm using to prop up my music isn't helping matters.

Day Nine

Another long day before I get to the flute. The warm up exercises and scales are going well. I can find all the notes (with the help of my crude fingering chart) and hope to be able to do it without the chart by the time of my next lesson. I turn to 'The Prince of Denmark' with new enthusiasm but still end on that low D with a breathy wheeze. My sound is sometimes there, a fleeting moment when my lungs are filling as they should and my lips are forming a more focused airstream.

I sang in secondary school so I must have known how to breathe to some degree. I played one of the gondoliers in a school production of Gilbert and Sullivan's comic opera. In an all girls convent we 'male' leads were directed to stand with a manly hands on hips posture and belt out our numbers. Mine was 'Take a Pair of Sparkling Eyes'. The 'females' stood demurely, cupping one hand into the other as they sang. I remember the nerves and exhilaration of waiting behind the heavy velvet curtain with a packed assembly hall beyond, the thrill of being in the school at night, backstage with lurid makeup and high pitched squeals. Later I sang with choirs; then there were long years with no singing, beyond an occasional karaoke session. I didn't know the full lyrics of any one song. I'd slowly started singing again at parties in the house of good friends. Liam would play his guitar and the singing could continue until dawn: everything from sheet music to Googled lyrics, virtuoso piano players, accomplished singers and enthusiastic tryers. Guitars and music in a friendly room around a groaning table of wonderful food. Making music, singing to a room of listening friends, felt like huge fun, although at first it was terrifying.

Back at the flute classes Marie has written a one word instruction into my notebook in capitals. 'RELAX,' it reads. This is easier said than done.

Day Ten

We are a third of the way through my thirty days and while I can follow a simple piece of music and make a tune, my breathing is still not great. My sound comes and goes like a wave. Sometimes the second rendition of a piece is better than the first, which tells me I need to relax a little bit more from the first note. My brain is working to remember where to position my fingers in order to get certain notes and as I repeat the bars it gets easier to change between them in time. Tonight I watch with my heart thumping while my eldest stands up with his violin in front of a hot school hall full of parents at his first school concert. It is almost unbearably moving to see him and his friends standing tall and proud and playing notes in time together on their small violins.

The recital starts with a tune sung by a few voices, then more voices, then a few violins and finally all the violins and voices with a cello and piano accompaniment by their teachers. Nobody fluffs anything or drops their bow or buckles with nerves. They are in proud performance mode. Hot tears roll down my cheeks.

On the way to the school my son had said he felt butterflies fluttering up from his stomach into his throat. 'Those are good,' I told him. 'They will help you play and make you feel more wonderful afterwards than you would if you just didn't care.'

He nods. 'Yeah,' he mutters, 'just a silly old boring concert,' trying out studied insouciance. We both know this is not what he's feeling.

Afterwards I have to tear off late for a dinner reviewing a restaurant. I spend the first ten minutes breathlessly trying to convey to my dining companion how wonderful this first concert was. I sound like every other proud parent who ever lived.

Day Eleven

It's tall and green and a sign that we are becoming a musical household. I could have bought a bright yellow one or a pink one but I choose the bright green music stand in a city centre shop. I also buy a book of flute arrangements of classics, movie themes and pop songs. 'The Girl from Ipanema' looks doable but proves trickier when I try it. The problem with pop songs is that they sound so cheesy on the flute, like those 'hooked on classics' recordings with clapping behind classical pieces. Offenbach's 'Barcarolle' is there too, in a different key but nearly playable. I'm thinking I will practise it and try to play it for Marie at tomorrow's lesson. It has plenty of C sharp to middle D combinations. To play the first note you have to lift all your fingers off the keys, leaving only the little finger of the right hand on a small key at the bottom. For the D several more fingers go on. It's tricky to keep the flute balanced but it's starting to feel slightly more natural.

I have a new respect for classical musicians. It is both inspiring and daunting to hear Marie, a concert flautist, talk about practising for several hours in advance of a concert. The human urge to make music is one thing; the dedication to spend hours quietly practising in a room by yourself takes another set of skills. I'm finding my ten and fifteen minute sessions more relaxing and come back to my computer screen feeling centred and ready to work.

Day Twelve

'Your breathing is appalling,' Marie says, as my shoulders shoot up to my ears and the gasp of air in the top of my lungs collapses my sound. I am realising how ambitious the 'Barcarolle' is. 'Let's try your favourite tune,' Marie says, crossing out the repeat bars to give us both a break. I've a feeling I'm going to hate this tune by the end of my efforts.

Learning to breathe differently is feeling impossible. As an experiment I have been asking several people to take a deep breath. Most of them do what I do, throw back their shoulders and puff out their chests, like Popeye in the old cartoon when the spinach hits his system. But this is a breath with lots of bluster and no ballast. It's all wrong for playing the flute. I need to imagine the air going much deeper into my lungs, breathe down to my knees, trying to visualise filling my stomach with air. I remember a long forgotten model of a diaphragm, the muscle dipping down like a smile, creating the vacuum in the lungs to fill them deeply, top to bottom. I think I might have seen a model with a bell jar and a rubber plate at the bottom in a long forgotten biology lab. I seem to remember you could pull the 'diaphragm' down and watch two tiny balloon lungs expand as the air was pulled into them.

In real breathing, as the diaphragm pulls down it squashes the stomach, making the belly balloon out. It is a motion that is everything the 'shoulders straight stomach in' school of ladylike deportment opposes. I think of all those women in corsets whose diaphragms could never operate as they were caged in by whalebone and elastic that allowed only the top of the lungs to function. Little wonder that vials of smelling salts were frequently the corset wearer's accessory.

I can take a deep breath and let it out slowly but as soon as I raise the flute to my lips and try to form a good *embouchure* I start breathing into the top of my lungs. They burn, the breath is gone in a gasp and I'm dizzy and light headed trying to reach the end of a phrase. I'm beginning to realise that when I'm under pressure my body responds by taking shallow breaths. Knowing what you're doing wrong is one thing. Fixing it when your body has been responding to stress in this way for two decades is another. I watch my son take a deep breath to blow a hand made windmill. His shoulders stay where they are and he breathes deeply as naturally as any classically trained singer.

This exercise has become as much about learning to breathe as learning to play. I'm just not sure such a big thing is achievable in thirty days. It's about unlearning decades of shallow breathing, the kind of breathing known in singing circles as 'the breath of exhaustion'. Whether that means it exhausts you or it's the kind of breathing you do when too exhausted to breathe correctly is hard to know.

The idea of holding ourselves in, the engagement of the core, has been a feature of women's deportment, from whalebone corsets to worries about muffin tops over low rise jeans. That rounded soft belly and the thickening of the lower ribs is culturally *verboten*. It's yet another reason to hate the fashion world and its obsession with skinny waifs. By breathing down into our lower lungs we are breathing better. I think of how a baby's tummy lifts and falls as they breathe. We are born knowing how to breathe. We lose it along the way.

This is becoming more of a physical challenge than an intellectual one. If I could get someone else to blow and just learn to finger the notes, I could master it in thirty days. A eureka moment around now would be good.

Day Thirteen

I get not a eureka moment but an epiphany. I'm sitting in a darkened theatre – the Pavilion in Dun Laoghaire – listening to one of my favourite sounds, evocative of childhood and memories of anticipation and a sense of special occasion. An orchestra is tuning.

For many years my dad played double bass with the Dublin Baroque Players, an amateur orchestra made up of great characters. I remember these musicians as grown ups with the sound and colour turned up. They seemed to live at full pelt, whether storytelling or playing music or having friendships or fun. Our first family holiday abroad, when I was eight, was an orchestra trip to Spain. I remember one venue where the sounds of the Dublin orchestra drifted out into a long Spanish evening and the swallows screeched through the sky as if choreographing their flight to the notes.

Tonight the orchestra's flute player is my teacher, Marie, and her long notes are hanging silvery and beautiful over the top of the other notes as the musicians get their instruments and their bodies in tune for the performance. The sound is a flurry of discord and disparate trills and scales and long notes before they all come together under the conductor's baton. Once again I am small and safe and warm, sitting beside my mum at a performance. She would be wearing her good jewellery, a charm bracelet and Chanel Number 5, and her eyes would shine as she watched an opera, following every phrase as closely as you might read the lines of a book.

She's beside me again tonight and we are watching a wonderful production of Verdi's *La Traviata*, the story of doomed love that can leave its audience wrung out and weeping by the end. It's got some of opera's most beautiful tunes. The ground level stage is so close that it feels like as if we as audience members are part of the dazzling parties and toe to toe with the characters in the Paris garret.

It is the perfect place to watch the singers breathe, deep belly breaths that never raise their shoulders. Their lungs as bellows feed the sound of their voices and allow them to fill every corner of this auditorium with music. Soprano Sinead Campbell Wallace is an impressive Violetta. She commands the fiendishly difficult melodies, showing her years of voice and breath training. The last notes are as beautiful as the first. I can't take my eyes off the young women singers, chorus and main parts. They stride around the stage breathing down to their toes and sending their voices soaring over our heads. I sit in my seat breathing properly, deeply. On the way home I stop the car and look out over Dublin Bay, breathing long properly deep breaths of the summer air. It is exhilarating and hilarious. Here I am, forty one years old, learning to breathe properly. Two shapes bob in the water. I watch them carefully. An arm rising shows they are people, not seals. Night swimmers.

Over the weekend each practice session is better. I can hear when my breathing is not good and my *embouchure* starts to dry and wheeze as I get tired. At my next lesson Marie is relieved by my progress and she plays an accompaniment on the piano for the first time. We are at the midway point and I am starting to believe I will be able to do this. It's already been so much more enjoyable and so much more frustrating than I could have imagined.

Day Twenty Two

There are eight days left. And I still can't play any of my pieces without a gasp in the wrong place or a fluffed note. Technically I can make musical notes come out of the flute but musically it's a long way off. 'Make it sing,' Marie says to me at the lesson this morning. It's that mystical thing of 'expression', playing a sequence of notes in a way that communicates the feeling of the music, that essential heart of a piece that can bring tears to our eyes or make us feel fleetingly lifted and happy. It's not the flat technical ability of *la la la;* of hitting each note in time, but linking them, through tone and volume, into an arc of feeling. A Monday morning dash to the suburbs, late for my lesson as always, is not the best way to start this week of weeks when we will try to cram in the rest of my musical education and finish with a four piece performance medley. Gershwin's 'Summertime' is definitely on the list. I've been singing it to my boys at night for years. It's a simple but challenging enough piece, requiring more breath than I can manage on a first run through to make those long notes sing.

I'm tempted to leave the flute in its case today. This morning's lesson was exhausting and I feel I need a break. But I change my mind and take it out of the case to give 'Summertime' a run through. It's still rusty but I can see that it's doable. Tomorrow's session will be all about learning it by rote. The dog is shooting me doleful glares. Two things make her leave my side – the hair dryer and the flute. And there's been an awful lot of flute recently.

Day Twenty Three

I am sitting in a packed concert hall where my middle son and his four year old friends are playing violins. I have rushed here to join them with my flute. But they are playing something very complicated and I can't seem to catch the note or find my place. I can't see the music and I am lost. Suddenly I remember I have left my other two children at home alone to come and do this. I rush outside, panicking. I'm on Grafton Street trying to find a taxi and realise I have no money. At a bank machine I find a bundle of sterling notes wrapped in plastic and hand them to a man I know is a drug dealer. I still have no money to get home to my abandoned children.

So here's my first anxiety dream about what I am planning to do in four days' time. When Marie asked me how I would like to mark the thirtieth day of my flute challenge I shrugged and muttered something about small private triumphs. 'This is just for me. It's personal. I'll know that I can play and that's all that it's about.' So we decided we would record me playing something in the privacy of her music room and be done. The next day I have a change of heart and send out texts and emails inviting friends to the Iveagh Gardens at lunchtime on the thirtieth day for a small recital. My heart thumps faster as I send the texts. And the anxiety dreams start.

At a Friday morning lesson, my second last lesson before the performance, I have another minor breakthrough. By leaning forward I can keep my barrel of air working more efficiently and improving my *embouchure* allows me to reach the high notes without making them screech like nails on a blackboard. This shift in posture also helps the air to last longer. I can occasionally hear a hint of that warm golden sound that Marie has been talking about but as soon as I get it the sound goes again.

When my lungs are filled with enough air and the *embouchure* is good it's getting there. I still have trouble playing through a piece without fluffing a note but it's becoming more instinctive to move from one note to another.

I realise I am concentrating more than I do on almost any other aspect of my normal daily tasks. Reading music is not just about reading the notes as you're playing them, but about looking ahead to see what's coming next and using what feels like another part of your brain to prepare to play it. It requires the kind of focus I've lost from a lot of what I do. As I write or cook or play with my children

I am apt to break away and try to do something else simultaneously. Multi tasking is part of modern life and modern parenthood. We check our emails at the school gate, half listen to a voice on the other end of the phone as we read something on a screen in front of our eyes. If I am going to play this metre of silver plated nickel in any convincing way I am going to have to do it with tunnel vision and focus and unitask like never before.

Day Twenty Eight

I go to the Japanese shop Muji to buy a folder for my recital. I find this shop comforting in an entirely unrealistic fashion: it is full of minimalist plastic and grey fabric things, promising to give you a clean life, put every piece of clutter into a beautifully designed cubbyhole just for it, a life where you will never have to tear around an untidy house looking for something, but waft from one organised corner to another in grey pinstripe slippers. The folder is made from recycled plastic and has a clear sleeve for each piece of music, including my horribly annotated version of Damien Rice's 'Cannonball', picked out on a keyboard and written down to play while accompanied by Liam on guitar. In a few months' time, *X Factor* producers will have rediscovered this tune too. But in the meantime it's becoming our party piece, a guitar and flute duet.

Day Twenty Nine

The final lesson. Marie picks me up on my rhythm, which is far from good, and reminds me of the old trick of 'tea and coffee', tea for the crochets, coffee for the quavers. She points out the signatures at the start of pieces and gets my rhythm slightly more back into line.

In an era of *Glee* and *X Factor* and singalong karaoke it's easy to see music as something casual and there aboutish. We know the tunes and their rhythms, there or thereabouts, and we sing along as best we can, slurring the words and la-la-ing through the lyrics we don't remember. But there is a precision and a rigour to learning to play sheet music, playing every note the way the composer wrote it down, not sliding or skimming it but enunciating it clearly, rhythmically and with the purity it requires. Taking its rhythm seriously suddenly gives the Gershwin 'Love Is Here To Stay' sense. Without it I'm stringing the notes, hitting them accurately but without any sense of the music of the piece, its jaunty joy. Gershwin tunes are a marriage of rhythm, lyrics and melody and taking a one without the other approach turns them into something so much less than what was intended.

We record the pieces as Marie plays along on the piano. It's a new joy to play with an accompaniment. It feels less exposed but is more exacting in terms of keeping a strict rhythm. The sound quality on the recording is horrible, but not as horrible as the recording of my first lesson. Six hours of lessons and the thirty days are nearly over. I've enjoyed almost every minute of this exercise, even when it felt like failure.

Day Thirty

It's suddenly happening. I've packed my music stand into a backpack and I'm off to the Iveagh Gardens on my bike. I've run through the pieces and they've done their usual job of surprising me with bursts of competence and passages of ineptitude. In many ways this has been a case of thirty days to mediocrity. I am far from a good flute player. I've no idea what nerves are going to do to my breathing. I have to remember to shove my shoulders down to my heels and breathe as if my rib cage is a barrel. I'm calm in a nerves honed to one thing kind of way. The sun is shining, which means the park will be packed. I tell myself I just have to do this for ten minutes in front of people who will be more than supportive if I only manage to wheeze out a few tunes. I've a feeling I am going to be blushing purple. I'm too nervous to eat and stuffed up with a cold.

The Iveagh Gardens are busy, full of strolling people in suits, shouting children and loungers on the grass, looking as if they're going to stay for the afternoon. I've put my music stand up and already feel conspicuous carrying it to the far end of the sunken lawn, where we're away from some of the crowds. Two friends are there when I arrive. I feel as exposed when I get the flute out as if I had just started undressing in public.

Normally in a quiet room I would do my tone exercises and

get things right before starting to play. Here it feels silly to be blowing disconnected notes as people look at me expectantly and I worry about park keepers arriving to cite some bylaw prohibiting unlicensed musical performances. In these circumstances it's best to wade straight in. I try a few brief notes, then launch into Greig's 'Morning'. At one stage the wind blows across the headpiece as I'm blowing one way and we cancel each other out. There's at least one fluffed note but I get through. The second piece, Gershwin's 'Love Is Here To Stay', is marked by the music stand falling over. Liam steps in to hold things together and I notice a man in a suit standing on the edge of the gathering beaming at me. He looks delighted to see someone playing music in this beautiful park.

I'm instantly horribly self conscious and nervous but by the end I'm starting to relax and do an almost passable rendition of Ennio Morricone's 'Gabriel's Oboe', the familiar theme from the movie *The Mission*. The friends applaud, as expected. My teacher Marie looks happy. She's arrived on my invitation, after threatening to come and hide behind a tree. I'm tempted to ask her to play my flute just to show the small audience how it should sound but I don't want to give her my horrible cold as a parting gift. Slowly the park empties, except for us and the loungers. Seagulls and sunshine are overhead. It's one of those dream days that Dublin throws up occasionally. My boys arrive with their minder and we run around on the grass happily. Even though this has just been a friendly gathering it feels great to have got it over with. The next time I play in public will probably be after a dinner, with wine and people drowning out the flute as they sing along. In the meantime I will keep doing this quietly and privately on the landing in my house where the music stand now lives. The music will happen in between life's busier moments and maybe in the garden when the sun shines and the wind has stilled.

After the thirty days ended I continued to play the flute almost every day, sometimes just for a few minutes, sometimes for longer. There wasn't always an oasis of peaceful time to flute, so I would take my music stand into the bathroom as the boys were in the bath and practise as they splashed happily. As the potatoes boiled for dinner I would squeeze in a song or two. I could play songs that I sang to them, like 'Moon River' (a song that I think must be about death and the way we follow the long slow line of it every step) and 'Somewhere Over the Rainbow' and they would recognise them. Several family members have had a flute rendition of 'Happy Birthday' in the months since the thirty days ended. At my son's fifth birthday party I played for my first audience since the Iveagh Gardens. Even though the children had an average age of four I was still nervous, stumbling through 'Darth Vadar's Theme' ('Imperial March') from *Star Wars* as they scrambled around in a game of musical cushions.

Then with a dry mouth and pounding heart I lifted the flute to my lips at our Christmas drinks party in early December, playing 'Cannonball', some carols and a few Beatles numbers to enthusiastic singalong accompaniment. It was thrilling and vaguely show offy. At an even more musical party I played with three flute players, two teenage girls and another very accomplished player. The sound of four flutes harmonising on Christmas carols was wonderful and I beamed with the pleasure of being part of this impromptu band. The other three were better players than me but a year earlier I would have been sitting listening instead of being part of the music.

Public performances are a small feature of my rudimentary musicianship. This is something that has repaid my time and effort in spades. It wasn't inexpensive. Between the cost of the flute (€575) and lessons (€300) it was the priciest of all my ventures. But it reawakened a skill I hadn't used in more than twenty five years. It taught me to take a truly deep breath. And it gave me an escape hatch from daily reality into a slipstream of music, some of it centuries old, that feels restorative and meditative. When you are playing music you are in that musical moment, part of something intrinsically human. You are creating something, albeit in an amateur fashion and, in my case, primarily just for myself. But I'm creating it rather than consuming it.

It's also given me a chance to listen to music differently, to marvel at the discipline and ingenuity and sheer human grit and pig iron it takes to become a virtuoso musician.

Many of us learn music as children, trailing heavily into lessons with a sense of duty rather than possibility. Then teenage rebellion kicks in and the music books and instruments are shelved to gather dust. Even friends who kept on studying through their teens talk of putting their musical lives to one side as work and family soak up time. We stop producing music and become passive consumers. We watch the hopes and dreams of young singers on reality TV shows, watching them make their 'journeys', our own having hit a dead end years ago. Then someone has the nerve to start a singsong (a delicate social moment in any gathering) or like me you look at your children starting to learn music and feel a twinge of envy and regret, that moment when you think, 'I wish that was me.'

It takes more than thirty days to learn to play the flute. It's something I could continue to do for the rest of my days. And I'm still a jelly legged shallow breathing wreck when I play in front of anyone other than family. But an intensive start got me over the impossibility of those first stages into a basic level of competence. As an adult, learning and practising is a pleasure for me rather than a tiresome duty. The great discovery is that music waits for those of us who walked away from it all those years ago into what looked like a much more exciting world. It's still there in quiet dusty corners and the pleasure you can get from it is astonishing. Taking it up for the first time or returning to it as an adult relearner puts you back into a simpler time, an ordered and rigorous place. When it works, music can make life chime and harmonise in a way you wouldn't believe possible.

I am a fluter. Hear me flute.

2

Wasteland to Garden

It wasn't what sprang to mind when you heard the word 'garden'. Weaver Court was a partly concreted urban wasteland hemmed in by apartment buildings and roads and a terrace of Victorian two up two downs.

This place has history. Decades ago it was from a house nearby that a criminal family, commonly blamed for bringing heroin to the city, ran their business. Weaver Court was the site of a public housing complex of thirty six flats built in the 1960s. It's a familiar story of public housing failure. Former residents remember a place of comfort and comparative luxury when the flats were first built and a community of friends and neighbours.

But the complex, like so many others, fell into disrepair and failed. In 2008 it was torn down with the intention of building anew. Then the private developer funds to build a better housing scheme were blasted away by the economic downturn. So this site sat like a blot on the cityscape, like so many other 'mothballed' sites around Anglo's Ashes Ireland. A high slate grey iron palisade fence was built around it to keep everyone out. Scruffy grass grew, defecating cats slunk through the railings and beer and vodka bottles were slung over for target practice.

But now there were plans to take it from dereliction to garden. On a sunny Monday morning I sat in a windowless meeting room talking to two city council officials about the logistics of the project. The legal department was drawing up a lease, allowing people who wanted to garden this space to rent an allotment – a simple eleven month lease.

By breaking the lease for one month a year the city council retained ownership for some future redevelopment. It's a model that could be applied to any of the derelict NAMA sites around the country.

Outside, men with diggers were breaking up the last of the concrete slab and exposing the soil. Later trucks dumped topsoil about a foot deep on the ground. The soil came from a football pitch in Leixlip in Kildare where they were laying AstroTurf. Post and wire fencing divided the site into twenty eight allotments and a larger community garden plot and it was nearly ready to go.

Almost a year earlier a group of neighbours in the area where I live had worked to get a tiny long padlocked park opened up for everyone to use. The city council agreed to let a resident living on the square become a key holder and lock the park morning and night. In the months since the gate was first opened Rosary Park in Oscar Square had become a meeting place for children, parents, dog walkers and neighbours. Although it was nothing more than a few patches of grass, with cherry trees and a statue in the middle, it was now a social space, despite long held fears that it would become a magnet for antisocial behaviour.

Those of us who were lucky enough to get drawn in the allotment lottery would be getting a key to Weaver Court. Another disused public space was going to be put into the hands of the people who lived around it, most of whom had little or no garden space of their own. The key to the gate would also unlock the container shed for tools and the hose for watering. In return I handed over €82 (the balance of the calendar year's rent of €150 as we were already well through the calendar year) and signed a lease agreement.

It was an experimental project. I could tell that the city council had some concerns that this place was too much on the front line of the inner city to succeed. This was gardening in the ghetto. There was an unspoken fear that the sight of a group of organic gardening types would provoke anger and hostility from people outside the fence. It was the first time the council had developed a brownfield site as allotments (as opposed to a greenfield site within a park). There was a lot riding on this.

I was a novice gardener. Two small raised beds in the back garden had so far produced some spindly carrots and just about enough peas for one meal. In an old postage stamp yard in my first house I once got a bumper crop of cherry tomatoes. They ripened, then rotted while I was away on an extended trip.

The key to my allotment would be coming at a time when I had enjoyed a small gardening triumph. Tired of buying supermarket coriander plants, taking off the plastic sleeve and watching them wilt and die hours later, I had repotted one with plenty of compost and put it in the sunniest spot outside, where it thrived. Along with the unkillable crop of chives (which had survived the previous two winter snowfalls) and a mint plant, these herbs constituted my growing success so far this year.

Allotments are the apartments in Bulgaria of post boom Ireland. Everyone wants one. A city council official told me how in his allotment project, in Crumlin, three men who had lost their jobs had thrown their time and hearts into their large bare patches of field with fantastic results. His nearest allotment neighbour was a woman in her seventies who was thriving like her plants.

The allotment craze has its fair share of celebrity enthusiasts. Stella McCartney once called a slouchy purple patent handbag planted with lettuce, lemon balm and thyme a 'micro allotment', to show how little space you need to grow food. Two months before I got my key Michelle Obama had been photographed planting the White House vegetable garden on the South Lawn with a group of primary school children. It was the third season for the garden, which is in raised beds on the manicured lawn. That season she was growing spinach, peas, lettuce, Swiss chard, leeks, blueberries, raspberries and herbs as part of her 'Let's Move' programme to fight childhood obesity. The First Lady's gardening project has prompted a new interest in growing vegetables in the US, although some argue it's just window dressing to avoid squaring up to big food companies in advance of an election.

At 45 square metres my plot in the Weaver Court allotments was bigger than anything I had ever gardened before. I didn't have an army of gardeners who could quietly tend the patch every day and it was already well into the growing season.

The week before I got the key Weaver Court was still a hostile place. Icy winds and sharp pellets of stinging rain whipped down as I took my first walk into the site and tried to imagine it as it would be a few weeks later, full of people and plants. As with any big project the last stages of preparation seemed to take for ever. The previous week I had written an article for *The Irish Times* about restaurants that were growing their own food in kitchen gardens. I had been struck by the enthusiasm of people I interviewed, many of them novice gardeners. Two of the spaces were borrowed gardens, now providing masses of just picked food and learning opportunities.

Day One

Standing on Patch 12 in the middle of the site I looked down at my small flowery handled trowel and thought of Roy Scheider's line when he first spots the shark in *Jaws*: 'We're gonna need a bigger boat.' Knowing my allotment's rough dimensions on paper and seeing them for the first time in reality were two very different things. On that opening day a plant sale organised by the city council helped to take the bare look off this large patch of rough, lumpy brown soil. I bought a dozen spindly leeks (more like spring onions), six Swiss chard plants and a dozen cheerful green pak choi. Even this volume of plants looked like doll's furniture arranged at the edge of a ballroom.

The opening afternoon also gave me a chance to meet some of my new allotment neighbours, everyone friendly and keen as mustard, with a mixture of gardening abilities. This was to be as much about people as plants, so chatting would have to be factored into gardening time. It was a timely week to start growing food, with the story of killer cucumbers marching across Europe. In the end cucumbers were not the culprits but the scare raised serious questions about the food chains bringing us salad ingredients that could easily be grown in back yards or on balconies.

Plenty of local residents who weren't going to take on an allotment came to the plant sale. 'I'll just have to make sure the dog doesn't turn vegetarian,' one woman joked, as she bought some lettuces to plant on her balcony.

Within a few hours the greening of the site had started, with people putting their plant purchases straight into the soil. The space had suddenly become ours and many people left their new plants just inside the boundary of their allotment, ready for planting at a later date. Something small seemed to shift. Already this inner city wasteland was taking on a different character.

Then it was back home on the bike to relieve the child minder and throw on the dinner. Later that evening I brought my eldest boy, who has been gardening with my father since he was able to walk, to see our new allotment.

It felt enormous, bare and beautiful, but huge. By that stage in the evening the pessimist in me could see it sprouting weeds around plants shrivelling from drought. There was very little shelter, with no tall buildings near enough to cast shadow, so that the sun, when it shone, would beam down from early to late. Any dry spell would mean plenty of hefting water from the tap to the beds.

I thought about resting parts of it, growing green manure to be dug in to provide nutrients in the areas not growing food. The wire fencing that marked the plot looked perfect for peas to scramble up.

My son and I began the dirty work of getting pot bound plants out of their plastic containers and into the ground. It was astonishing how much birdsong there was in this early summer twilight. Birdsong, car alarms and distant sirens were the strangely soothing sounds of an inner city gardener.

I remember thinking if the summer kept up like this working in this garden in the evenings would be a pleasure, a relaxing break from the Bermuda triangle of desk, hob and sink. There would be days when it might feel more like a chore but that first evening was not one of them. We came home with dirt under our nails. It had embedded itself into one of my rings, obscuring the tiny stones in a crust of good honest dirt.

Day Two
It was a day of tearing from one thing to the next: writing, recording an interview, buying ingredients for a chocolate biscuit cake for my eldest boy's birthday party. I made the cake with three boys to

help – it turns out their expertise at breaking things makes them perfect helpers for a cake involving broken biscuits. Then we were invited to a surprise party that night so my gardening hour had to be winkled into the schedule. I wasn't very motivated as I headed off on my bike with a watering can in the basket. But when I got there a young family, mum, dad and daughter, were gardening like mad and grinning at the pleasure of it.

I brought bright blue mohair wool and some sticks, something that I had woken up thinking about that morning. I couldn't find the measuring tape in the rush to get out of the house so I paced the plot instead, measuring a pathway down the centre of my rectangle and eight roughly equal planting areas, four on each side of the path, marked out with blue wool. Suddenly I had what this garden needed: a plan. I replanted the hastily planted leeks, pak choi and Swiss chard to get them into their zones.

I realised after a while that I had forgotten to bring my phone. I didn't miss it. The absence of that small lump in my pocket added to the sense of peace and escape. I decided to move some space hungry cauliflowers out of the small raised beds at home and put them in here where they could stretch their roots and breathe under this sunny, wide city sky.

Day Three

After some more light gardening I picked my eldest up from his play date. He had spent it on a nearby allotment project, where a community group has been successfully farming food from raised beds for a few growing seasons. He was pink with effort, exhausted, muddy and happy. They had beds full of potatoes, one patch grown by a Simon Community project, giving homeless people a chance to garden. They had scarecrows, barrows and impressive tools for rooting out weeds. It felt like a more bedded in version of what we were doing nearby.

Day Four

It was another hectic dashing around kind of day and by the end of it I had half my cauliflowers in the allotment and half back in the raised beds at home. It was hot and dry and the grey green leathery leaves of the cauliflowers were wilting. By the time I got to the allotment the transplanted cauliflowers had sagged to the ground in defeat under a blazing sun. I gave them a good soaking and hoped it wasn't too late. As it turned out these were some of the few hot days that summer.

Day Five

It was my son's eighth birthday party and he looked a ringer for Harry Potter in the robes and fake glasses and wand his grandmother had bought for him. A painted red lightning scar on his forehead completed the transformation. I brought my parents to see the allotment with all three boys (and dog) in tow. They were impressed by the space and the sense of communal effort. My dad mentioned raking before planting. The soil was full of clods and stones and I realised there was lots of heavy work to do here before we could really start to grow things.

Day Six

The last of the cauliflowers were transferred to the allotment in muddy batches in my bicycle basket. I sowed sorrel, basil and Florence fennel in their place in the raised beds. I also found some old pea and bean seeds that I decided to plant in the allotment. My muscles were aching from the digging and earth moving. Digging is a word we journalists often use to describe what we do but it's nothing like the real thing, that physical heft and heave of a shovel slicing through soil and lifting it. Soil is heavy, even dryish soil, like the kind we had in the allotment. And I was going to have to move a lot of it to get the place into shape.

Day Seven

A family trip to the garden. The dog and the two year old wrecked the blue mohair wool lines by trampling through them. Their dad removed the two younger boys and I set to work digging out a path with the eldest. He's always loved digging. Now he can do it with a proper spade and grown up purpose.

I met another near neighbour, Dee, who had arrived with crates of sprouted salad leaves. She insisted that we take some salad plants and spinach as she had so much. She had hung a sign on her tools in the container, encouraging people to borrow them if they wanted. After a good digging session that left my arms aching we decided to head home. 'Can I come again tomorrow?' my eldest son asked later. His enthusiasm was a tonic.

Day Eight

With my four year old in the back seat for company I drove to Templeogue to pick up some Jerusalem artichokes that have crowded out their owner's garden and that he had put up on the dublinwaste site as a freebie. The website is full of gardening bits and pieces that people no longer need. 'Miss Artichoke', the man said, smiling, as he answered the door of the suburban semi. He handed me a black sack of knobbly, dirt crusted artichokes sprouting pale green shoots.

Back at the allotment I finished off the main path with my eldest digger son. I used the shovel and he took the lighter, smaller spade. We got into a rhythm, slicing down, putting the weight of our bodies on to the lip of the tool. We soon realised that small loads were easily moved, instead of trying to heft a huge back straining amount. We make a good digging team. I'm seeing twelve bays now rather than eight, with paths separating them so they can be worked from either side without having to step in. Across the way, John, an allotment neighbour, was busy shuttering in his growing areas with left over timber decking. We both checked Dee's patch. She has become the allotment guru in my head. It is compost delivery day tomorrow.

Day Nine

I never thought I would be excited about the sight of a tipper truck dumping its load. But I was cycling by at the moment twenty five tonnes of brown bin compost arrived and it was a wonderful sight.

This was fertiliser made from the contents of Dublin's brown bins, food scraps and mucky waste tumbled with woody material and rotted down. The city council had agreed to pay for the delivery of one load to get us off to a good growing start and there was something great about food waste being used to grow food. Now we had to heft it into our plots. I went down through my telephone contacts list trying to find a friend who had a wheelbarrow. I came up with nothing but the realisation that we are a generation as likely to own a barrow as we would a churn. We have just emerged from an era when few people did their own gardening: instead we employed men from eastern Europe who came equipped with their own tools and wheelbarrows to do it for us.

My Pollyanna glee at the idea of brown bin compost waned a bit as its physical reality hit home. It had been dumped right beside my plot and the fence strained with the weight of the stuff bulging through the square wire. It gave off a high hum of decomposition as the organic material continued to rot. In the coming days the smell would spread around the neighbourhood, announcing the arrival of the allotments in a way we really hadn't planned.

The local kids decided the pile of dark brown stuff was a mountain of elephant poo from Dublin Zoo. Others passing by said it was spent hops from Guinness's brewery nearby. Everyone had a theory. In fact it was a weird mixture of human detritus. People must put all kinds of things in their brown bins. There were shards of glass and plastic and the innards of a red biro, all tumbled together with plenty of woody bits of timber and cloudy sections of ash.

The heavy groundwork continued but I could see the lighter work in prospect. My seeds had arrived in the post from Irish Seed Savers in Clare, a brown envelope full of tiny plastic Ziploc bags with their contents labelled simply on the front. Prettiest were the Contender French Bush beans: hard skin coloured nuggets with swirls of brown. It was difficult to believe that these marble hard things would sprout soft green shoots. I was looking forward to burying them deep in a raked and composted bed and making a bamboo tripod for them to clamber up: a little light gardening as opposed to all this groundwork.

But that was still a way off and it hailed on me as I was digging that day. It didn't augur the best start to the growing season.

My hands were getting rough and sore and a tweet about the

state of them led gardening expert Jane Powers to tweet me the name of gardeners' gloves (Shola) and where I could buy them. It was an expensive link to an online gardening store. I spent €76 on two pairs of gloves and some fruit plants, including a golden raspberry variety that fruits in the autumn. With the €82 I'd paid for my allotment, €20 to Seed Savers and a tenner at the plant sale, we were on €186 and counting.

Day Ten

The compost was really stinking by now. The steamy stench penetrated our clothes. Liam could smell it from our skin, hair and boots when we arrived home.

My eldest son spent the session digging doggedly and chattering all the time. Down here it was easier to hear him, where there was no chorus of other brothers jostling for my attention. We had birdsong and car noises, a high up jet and the occasional siren. There was the clink of Dee's tiny essential oil bottles, hung on her wire fencing to scare the birds. It was smelly but peaceful.

Day Eleven

We tried to ignore the smell and get on with the planting. It seemed to be getting worse.

Day Twelve

It's a day away from the allotment at a family wedding and the sun shone from a fresh, puffy white clouded summer's day.

Day Thirteen

The heavens opened today and a biting, unsummery wind howled. The plants were drenched and the soil lost its dry, dusty look, turning a deeper brown down to the root level. I think I am starting to become a gardener, one of those annoying ones who looks out at a sodden grey day and says, 'Great to see the rain; the plants needed this.'

Day Fourteen

Today was one of those days when it felt as if I were ten minutes late for everything. That feeling of always being one step behind the clock rolled from one task to the next so by the time it came to the evening gardening session I was exhausted and not relishing an hour of bad smells and back breaking work. I hadn't had time to go the garden centre and buy the bamboo stakes I needed to mark my bean planting. But I pushed myself out the door for the short cycle to Weaver Court.

A lot of gardening had been done over the weekend and things were starting to take shape in the plots. No two plots were the same. In one of the last areas of concrete in the corner of the site there was a large, dried up weedy bush with strong branches. I used the tinder dry sticks to make my own pea and bean supports. I planted the beautiful seeds with a stick alongside each one that the new shoot could curl its soft tendrils around. It was all a bit Blair Witch meets *Blue Peter*, especially finished off with the blue mohair wool. But it was immensely satisfying to find something on this empty site that I could reuse to help this garden get growing.

Day Fifteen

We had our first allotment dinner today, well not quite a full dinner. I was at the halfway point of my thirty days and it was time to eat the first bit of allotment grown food. On the way back from the supermarket I picked some Swiss chard leaves. They were spinachy and tender and delicious fried, with a lemon butter sauce. In just over two weeks they had bulked out enough to allow me to pick some leaves. Again the allotment surprised me with its powers to relax and I filled a happy hour pottering. I had my eldest son with me and he was a bit worried that the interesting bit was finishing now that the heavy digging was done. 'It's hard to believe this was once a barren wasteland,' he said. He's right.

Day Sixteen

An empty attic water tank filled with compost at the front of a friend's house was the raised bed in which she was growing butternut squash. They had run out of space so we took two squash plants and replanted them in our allotment, where space was still something of which we had plenty. We also took two pepper plants. It was a risk transplanting them at this stage but so far nothing had died on me, even the badly traumatised cauliflowers. These were now growing well, their leaves taking on elephant ear proportions after wilting so badly initially.

My fruit plants arrived from the online garden centre in a large, heavy box. They looked healthy, with strong roots that curved round the outside of the compost root ball in an effort to stretch out and grow. It was a rare hot, sunny day, hot enough to need a sun hat and to have to take refuge in the shade of the large lorry container that acts as a shed.

I began to see some payback for all the digging. The soil in the raised areas we had created was easy to dig and a trowel or spade slipped down easily into the crumbly earth. Putting in new plants was pleasant work. The two blueberry bushes had some tiny green berries which would fill and turn purple and juicy.

Day Seventeen

I was beginning to look forward to a gardening session, as with any break from routine. There was the same sense of a peaceful haven, somewhere I would be trying to do just one thing. Even at the end of a long day of work and family life there was pleasure in pulling on the wellies and heading out the door. It was different from walking into the back garden where you were always on the elastic end of the needs of a child or a computer or a phone call or an unemptied dishwasher. The habit of not bringing my phone with me had stuck. This was a place where blackberries with a small 'b' were the only variety allowed.

At my book club later that day I discovered a couple of very keen gardeners amongst the friends I knew as book lovers. They were quietly growing cucumbers and tomatoes from seed, women with busy lives who fitted in summer gardening jobs. Maria, one of my oldest friends, who had invited me into the book club, promised me some plant cuttings from her garden: mint and horseradish. Another friend, Yvonne, was going to give me some cucumber plants. Good gardeners are generous because they have an abundance of produce.

Day Eighteen

It was coming up to the summer solstice, a time of the year when I would normally wonder where all those long evenings had gone. That point when we turn the corner into shortening days always seemed to come too soon in the summer for me. I would feel shortchanged as I hadn't been out in those long hours of daylight when the twilight lingers and it never gets fully dark. But not this year. I had been part of those long light filled evenings. They had allowed me to graft a daily gardening routine on to the end of a busy working day. It was a clever system. Just like plants, humans respond to light, so gardening has a rhythm that puts us back into that world of working outside for longer hours when the days are bright. And even in this cloud smothered island in the north Atlantic that midsummer light feels like energy from the sky.

Gardening was starting to make me appreciate our climate: its benign moods, regular downpours and rare golden sunny days. Once I was working I was warm, even on cooler evenings. Like all worthwhile pursuits, gardening was getting me outdoors even when I didn't particularly feel like it.

My peas and beans were planted and the waif and stray plants from Maria and Yvonne were all in. I had sown phacelia, a green manure crop, in the planting bay nearest the entrance to my plot and it was starting to spread a green carpet of frondy leaves. Now I had to cultivate that other great skill of a gardener. Patience.

Day Nineteen

Every visit to the allotment brought another conversation with someone inside or outside the fence. Plenty of people talked about how pleased they were to see the place becoming a garden. It quickly became a source of pride rather than a monument to failure. In all the hours I spent there I never felt any hostility from outside the fence. 'Would you grow us some weed, missus?' was a joke shouted fairly regularly by passing teenagers. We heard the news that the city council had approved another twenty one allotments on a similar site nearby.

My pea plants were starting to poke through, curled up leaves pushing their pointed tips into the light. After what had felt like a long wait, seeing pea shoots coming up so fresh and green was exciting. Again it seemed more than a little miraculous that they were emerging from the dried out stone hard pellets I'd pushed into the soil less than a fortnight earlier.

I was beginning to see that good gardeners are a lot like fashion designers. They think at least one season ahead. Just as catwalk models swelter in winter gear as the normal world dresses in T shirts, so gardeners are thinking about winter greens while the rest of us are getting to grips with summer produce.

Day Twenty

After the initial burst of excitement and activity, life on Weaver Court allotments settled into a pleasant rhythm. There were fewer sawing and building noises and less clinking of forks or shovels on stones as people dug over their soil. When I first thought about the gardening project I imagined going there in the early mornings, getting up when everyone else was asleep and putting in the work before the day started. But it has turned out that I'm an evening gardener. Others obviously worked to a different timetable as there were many gardeners I never met, I only ever saw their plots changing, landscaping done and plants reaching for the sky.

Then there were the people like Harry Jones, who spent many hours a day there. A Dubliner in his seventies, Harry had an old kitchen chair on a paving slab for his regular cigarette breaks. He always had time to talk and conversations with him were part of the pleasure of this place.

Harry was thirteen when he got his first job. In W. Drummond and Sons, the seed and garden supply shop, he told them he was fourteen so he could get in the door. Two years later he had to confess to a stony faced manager that he was a year younger than he had claimed. They let him stay on.

People still go into W. Drummond in Dublin's city centre. Only instead of seeds and plants they buy books. The company's Dawson Street shop is now Hodges Figgis and there is a bargain books basement where the seed potatoes and fertiliser were once stored.

Drummonds was just one of three huge gardening shops in the city centre in the 1950s. There was a large depot on Dame Street and McKenzies on Pearse Street. The gardening business was booming. All over the city families like Harry's had moved out of tenement buildings – he was born in a tenement in Holles Street – to suburban houses with front and back gardens. Today's boom in city gardening is a pale version of what happened then, when getting dinner from your garden was a routine part of life. If you had a family and a garden you grew vegetables at home.

Harry remembers delivering plants to Mia Farrow's mother, Maureen O'Sullivan (who played Jane in some of the Tarzan movies), when she lived on Killiney Hill. It was Christmas week and the Drummonds van got stuck and churned up the sparkling white gravel. A team went back the very next day, towed the stricken van and raked the gravel smooth again. It was different in those days, he said, like someone explaining life on another planet: there was a precision about how you were dealt with.

The new gardening boom is beginning to bring garden businesses back into the city centre. On the northside Mr Middleton on Capel Street sells flowers and food plants to apartment dwellers and people with small back gardens. On Cork Street the Urban Plant Life shop is a vast depot hidden behind a small street frontage. They've already seen a growth in demand for vegetables and seeds and are stocking up their food plant section.

Harry remembered the seed catalogue from when he was a boy worker in Drummonds. It was, to his eyes, a wondrous thing, full of the kinds of pictures that looked so real you could walk into them. I was curious about this piece of history so headed to the City Library reading room in Pearse Street where they have a copy of a Drummonds bulb catalogue from 1954, part of the wonderfully named Dublin Business Ephemera Collection. For its time it was lavishly illustrated, with colour plates and a cover photograph of a huge bed of flowers grown from bulbs, with instructions inside for how and when to plant the bulbs. Orders over a certain quantity were delivered free to any railway station so this Dublin shop was the heart of many a garden across the country. There was nothing new about what was happening in Weaver Court. As members of today's allotment generation we were just slowly relearning old skills.

Day Twenty One
It was a parenting fail for me today when I missed my eldest son's school sports day. He was upset not that I wasn't there to see him race against his friends but that I wasn't there to drive him home and he had to walk, exhausted after all his efforts, back to the school to be picked up.

Working at home is a juggling act. I try to make the school pick ups, leaving the other boys with the child minder at home so that I can whizz to the school gate by bike and keep in touch with the other parents. It's only very occasionally that I'm wearing anything that looks like work clothes so all those boundary setting actions like getting into a suit and walking into an office are missing from my routine. I am neither fish nor fowl in the black and white definition of a working or stay at home parent.

Day Twenty Two
Although we won't remember the summer of 2011 as a hot one it was quite a dry one, so at this stage watering was the bulk of the gardening work that needed to be done. There was a communal hose but it was tricky to get it hooked up so I did a lot of water carrying. It had a nice quiet rhythm of fill, carry, pour. I was lucky that the distance between tap and plot was short.

Things were growing and bolting, especially the salad crops. The pak choi was shooting up sunny yellow flowers that were attracting the bees but not helping the flavour of the leaves. I was beginning to realise that a dozen pak choi plants were about ten more than we needed. On a cut and come again basis, pulling the outer leaves rather than the entire plant, two pak choi could provide more than enough for a weekly helping. Any more than that and the younger diners in our house started to complain. 'Not pak choi again, Mum.'

The creamy rocket flowers looked nice in salads and added a fiery kick.

Day Twenty Three
I didn't get to the garden today. I was just too busy to fit it in.

Day Twenty Four
I brought my eldest son and his two friends to the allotment today. They happily climbed the mulch heap and played while I put in some gardening time. The French beans I had planted were struggling to get above ground level. Something was munching the leaves as soon as they sprouted from the tiny new stems. The broad beans were doing much better and I had finally got around to buying some proper bamboo stakes to build the teepee structures and sheltering supports they would need.

Day Twenty Five
I had to go to Galway to review a restaurant so the garden had to wait until the evening.

Day Twenty Six
Fiann Ó Nualláin from inspiringgardens.ie came along to give us a little allotment workshop. He is a practical guy and his approach was to look at what you've got and tell you how to make the best of it.

He gave us plenty of time and advice. Gardening is full of jargon, 'rotation planting' being one of the key phrases. He explained that it meant simply not sowing the same crop in the same area each time. So my planting bays would work if I could keep moving the planting scheme up one each time. Potatoes suck nutrients from the soil so they need to be in a new patch in year two. Peas and beans put nitrogen back in, he explained, so they can be planted where the potatoes were the previous year.

It has taken this long for me to figure out what a space this size should be used for. Two of my sons love fruit – they would eat their body weight in strawberries and raspberries – so I decided to grow a lot of those fruits on the allotment. Unfortunately it's a long term plan. We won't be eating anything much in the way of soft fruit until a couple of summers ahead.

Fiann took a look at my spindly blueberry plants and advised me to put them into plastic trugs (the containers gardeners use for carrying and lifting things). They love damp, acid soil so I should fill the trugs with acid compost and put drainage holes on the side. Also I should bury a slice of peat briquette in the soil to increase its acidity. The peat acts like a battery, slowly releasing acid into the soil.

His final piece of advice was to make a nettle tea by steeping nettles in a bucket. They would provide a rich nitrogen feed and deter aphids. They would also stink, he warned. And they truly did, as I found out a fortnight later when Liam thought the drains had blocked at home.

Day Twenty Seven

A day off gardening today: we headed to my parents' house in Wicklow. I was taking a new interest in my dad's poly tunnel and raised beds, where he grows potatoes, asparagus, globe artichokes, tomatoes and a fantastic crop of raspberries every year. As a child I helped plant and harvest a small field of raspberry canes one memorable year. We were paid per punnet for picking the fruit when it was ripe in the summer. We had to keep the family black Labrador out of the raspberry field as he would suck the fruit off the plants and eat them as we were picking. I had my fill of raspberries that summer. I hated raspberries with the passion of a child who truly understood the tedium of fruit picking for pocket money. It took about twenty years for that to be worked out of my system. Now they're my favourite summer fruit.

Day Twenty Eight

Liam headed off to Berlin on a business trip so I had my mum up to help out with the boys in the evenings. Once they were all in bed I put on my anorak and headed out the door, much to her bemusement. At this stage there was less heavy work to do; it was more a maintenance visit. The Jerusalem artichokes were doing exactly what my Google search said they would: growing to the sky like sunflowers. Gardening by Google meant I planted them in the right spot, on the northerly border: otherwise they would have thrown other areas into shadow. Once they were planted I will always have them, it seems. They keep growing whether or not you replant them: stray tubers left in the ground once the main crop has been harvested in November sprout again in spring.

Day Twenty Nine

I dug out four lavender plants that had grown enormous in the front garden and brought them over to put into the patch and offer to the community garden. They were in full flower so it was the worst possible time to transplant them and they didn't survive the move.

A good few people were now coming to work the community garden in the evenings. It was a great chance for people who didn't get an allotment to get growing. The conversations were about weather and plants, what's growing and what isn't. Talking about what people did for a living rarely, if ever, came up for discussion: one of the interesting things about this different social place.

Day Thirty

It was my eldest son's last day at school and my mother in law arrived to help with the boys so I was able to get to the garden. The bees were buzzing happily around my bolted pak choi and the start of purple flowers on the green manure crop. At the end of thirty days I still had to see any huge results in terms of food grown and eaten. It was far from picture catalogue perfect, with neat rows of unblemished vegetables. But I had made a garden from a rocky clod filled patch of Kildare soil trucked into a neglected patch of the inner city. It was a great time of the year to make such a start, when the days were long enough to make it a pleasure rather than a chore, a thing to enjoy rather than a duty for the 'to do' list.

Had I become a gardener in thirty days? I had definitely tapped into a rich vein of rewarding work. I had made lots of rookie mistakes and learned plenty of new things. I stood there in the middle of this experiment and smiled.

A few weeks later I came home, proudly cradling something

almost like a newborn. The eldest son whooped with amazement when he saw it. It was a cauliflower the size of a football that our city garden had produced like a rabbit from a hat. Until that evening I had assumed that my brutal treatment of the cauliflowers had resulted in massive leaves and nothing else. But when I peeled back the leaves at the heart there it sat, perfect and beautiful enough to take top prize in a country show. From zero to hero in twelve weeks. Some cauliflowers were the size of tennis balls, hidden in the paler green central leaves. Others, like my prize specimen, were huge. Back home I sliced it thinly, ate it raw, then fried some of the rest lightly in nut oil. There were eleven more babies where that one came from. Eventually the great cauliflower glut became a challenge and I bagged it up and gave it to anyone who wanted it.

Everyone's patch evolved differently. There were quirky ornaments and strings of CDs glinting in sunlight to keep the birds off seedlings. The most impressive arrival was a tall, elegant bronze sculpture that was delivered to the patch of yoga teacher Jett. The sculpture, 'Ladybird', stands on a plinth looking down at the vegetables, the top part of her head, where her eyes and nose would be, sculpted into a beak. She arrived, unexpectedly, as an act of contrition for a night on the tiles from Jett's partner, a sculptor.

We got to show both the sculpture and the cauliflowers off to the camera when TV3's Martin King arrived down to film a piece about the project. In 2010, as part of his work as a presenter on *The Morning Show*, he gardened an allotment in Airfield in Dundrum, taking it from bare ground to food basket in twelve weeks. So he knew his onions.

On an open day for the community garden beside our allotment, where volunteers can come twice a week to plant and weed and harvest, visitors and regulars cooperated to bed in more than fifty plants. A group of boys came in to help. They stayed for most of the afternoon, as thrilled as kids usually are to be getting their hands mucky helping out, and left with bags of cauliflower and spinach and Swiss chard to bring to their nans for tea.

In a final piece about the allotment project for the *Evening Herald*, I noted what I'd learned in the process: 'It's not just about gardening:

It's about meeting other people, sharing ideas, tools, seedlings, hints and knowledge. In any allotment scheme you'll have complete novices (like me), experts and people in between. The magic happens when you get to chat to your allotment neighbours. As each patch evolves it's very easy to spot the experts.

You only need one or at most two pak choi plants to feed a household. Any more than that and you'll be knee deep in yellow flowers as they bolt to the sky. This also applies to Swiss chard and wild rocket. Save allotment space for the slower growing space hungry plants like cabbages, potatoes, cauliflowers and courgettes. Grow salad crops in window boxes at home, where you can harvest the leaves once or twice a day in the growing season.

There's loads of free stuff out there. I spent roughly €170 on the allotment this year, between rent and buying plants and equipment. But much of what I grew I got for nothing. Try dublinwaste.ie and jumbletown.ie for gardening tools, spare plants and many other useful things. Cultivate gardening friends. They will always have extra plants they're delighted to see someone else taking on.

Start slowly: the first impulse will be to spend hours digging (you'll ache all over the next day) and fill the plot with expensive plants. But growing from seed (just sow a line of one crop rather than using the whole seed packet) allows you to control the flow of food. Try and figure out if you really need ten large heads of cauliflower (which will all be ready to eat at the same time) and plan things according to what you like to eat. Put your efforts into unusual types of vegetables – purple broccoli, yellow carrots, broad beans – that are expensive to buy.

Don't be intimidated by the work: see the allotment as something on the 'to enjoy' list rather than the 'to do' list. Like most things, little and often is the best approach, especially in summer when even just a few days away can see things get parched or swamped by weeds. I used the long summer evenings to get things done. Even on the nights I was tired it was a pleasure once I got there.

Finally, write things down. You'd be amazed how quickly you forget what was planted where and how well it did.'

3

When You Lose Yourself, Grab Your Heels

It felt as if my eyeballs were starting to sweat. I was one large open pore. My heart was pounding and there was a strong possibility that I was going to fall over, throw up or black out. The man beside me was sweating so profusely the liquid ran off his elbow in a steady rivulet on to his already soaked towel. The sound was like a tap trickling. This is the hell that is Bikram yoga.

I started doing this extreme yoga in a super heated room about six months after the birth of my second son, in 2007. Then Dublin's only Bikram studio was in a low ceilinged lock up garage behind a red brick Victorian street in Portobello. You got the reek of human sweat as you arrived at the top of the laneway. That first evening I saw a knot of people from the previous class gathered outside, steam rising from their bodies into the city twilight, as they sucked down water from plastic bottles. They looked like the survivors of an ordeal.

A visiting American teacher taught my first Bikram class. He was a tall chopstick thin man who looked as if he was made out of burnished rubber. Today was the best day of my life, he told me and the other first timers in the room. Tomorrow would be the most important day of our lives because that would be the day we would decide to come back. Some Bikram teachers take themselves and the yoga deadly seriously.

Bikram is a series of Hatha yoga poses done in a mirrored and carpeted room heated to 40°C. The heat comes from electric blast heaters mounted near the ceiling. At your first class the room feels hot and clammy even before the yoga starts. The thing that first hits your senses is the smell – sweat that has soaked into the carpet and is now evaporating into the air with a briny tang. Teachers usually warn new students that it will get hotter. By the midway point in the class the heat has thickened the air until it is a hot soup pressing in on you claustrophobically. It's enough to make you feel like vomiting or fainting or just running from the room out into the lightness of fresh air. The idea behind the heat is to allow stiff muscles to stretch but it's also an attempt to pin down the butterfly western mind. The Bikram belief is that the heat forces you to concentrate on what you are doing in order to get through the class. Getting through the ninety minutes in the 'torture chamber' pushes out the space in your mind for all the other concerns of the working day. And my first class was an ordeal.

I'd had some false starts with yoga. When I was an undergraduate there was a dismal class in a chilly sports hall in the British university where I did my degree. We sat cross legged listening to a woman in a pink cardigan who talked in breathy tones about how to breathe. There was some light stretching and I half remember chanting at the end. I raced back to the college circuit training classes, dabbled in karate, did a bit of running and put the yoga thing down to experience.

A decade before my first Bikram class, when I was working as the drugs and crime correspondent of *The Irish Times*, I leapt out of bed on my morning off and ran down to sit in the headquarters of the Merchant's Quay drug project. The project had just published its annual report, a set of figures on the city's chronic heroin problem and the efforts to help the people affected by it. I had missed the story. Under the rules of daily news scoops I should have got an advance copy of the report the day before its publication and filed it for that morning's newspaper. Instead I was playing catch up. I sat hunched in a ball of tension listening to the presentation, then interviewing drug addicts about their lives. Their words put things in perspective. My minor worries were dwarfed by their stories, the familiar pathway of neglected and damaged children growing into broken adults.

On the walk back to the office with my notebook full of despair and hope, my left leg seized. I gripped a wall in Temple Bar, in tears of pain. Passersby assumed I was drunk or drugged and crossed the road to avoid me. One woman recognised that I was in trouble and helped me across the road to the then newspaper offices on D'Olier Street. The company doctor diagnosed a severe back spasm. Later an MRI scan identified disc degeneration. Several people mentioned surgery. I was twenty seven and I had a back problem.

About two years later I found Rowan Hennessy, a young zen calm Iyengar yoga teacher, whose classes made yoga make sense to me. Since my college karate and circuit training days I had covered the range of fitness options, handed over large chunks of money for gym membership, pumped iron, did spinning classes and tried a laughable aqua aerobics session. After the initial novelty wore off, all of them bored me senseless and failed to show any dramatic results. These Iyengar yoga classes were the first to stretch and strengthen muscles I needed to keep my back strong without surgery. They began to correct years of bad posture, all that time spent hunching over computer keyboards, cradling a phone in one ear, as I took notes, storing my stress and anxiety in pockets of stiffness in my vertebrae. In Rowan's classes in a small cramped room above a shop I found something that worked. After a class I slept like a stone. My back pain eased, then disappeared. I started fitting a yoga class into my schedule every week.

Then my husband Liam and I moved out of Dublin and I was pregnant for the first time, commuting to my city newsroom job and wondering how life as a security correspondent could work with a baby around. My only experience of pregnancy yoga was back to the scenario of sitting on the floor in cardigans. As a typical first time mother I felt I was pregnant only in the hours I wasn't working. The rest of the time my pregnancy was getting on with things without much thought from me.

Several years, a swerve off the hard news career track and two babies later, I reeled out of my first Bikram class seeing stars and pinpricks of light in front of aching eyes. Cycling home I felt the cool evening air wash over me as if for the first time and with it a sense of calm. Something about the class had reminded me of labour: the lulls between effort, the deep sense of rest after it was finished. And just like labour there were many moments when I hated every second of it and wanted it all to stop. But something made me go back. I did the classes semi regularly for around six months, then the waters of two small children and a house renovation project closed over my head and I stopped going.

Anne Leonard is the woman who brought Bikram to Ireland. She trained in Los Angeles in 2002 and opened a studio in that garage in Portobello where I did my first class. In her first year of business she had a battle persuading sceptical Irish people of the merits of Bikram. Some classes had as few as two people. 'There were thirty four people in one class within six weeks of opening. But that was a peak,' she remembers. 'Then the troughs became fewer as more people became convinced.'

'People don't know [what it's about] for the first few classes. It depends on their lifestyle. One guy came in and said he just thought it was hell on earth. I remember speaking to him after class and saying he couldn't come in after two pints. He said, "Two pints? Try four bottles of wine." The whole idea is that it suctions your body back to its blueprint. So the more work you have to do the harder it's going to be.'

Leonard believes the effects of the yoga are simple: it forms a virtuous circle. It's too difficult to do a class after a night's drinking so people cut down on their drinking. Smokers find the classes hellish, she says, so they typically choose between their smoking habit and their yoga. 'I find the hardest clientele are those in their early twenties, the kids for whom nothing's gone wrong in their life,' she says. 'It's the people for whom something *has* gone wrong. Suddenly they have the clarity in their life about how to deal with it. Every class is an epiphany, something clicks or becomes clearer and you know where to go and what to do.'

Bikram has boomed in Ireland in recent years, which may be a by product of stress or people having more time. At the time of writing there were five Bikram yoga studios in Dublin, with seven more about to open: three in Dublin and one each in Athlone, Cork, Limerick and Maynooth.

Fitness fads have never been so popular or people so fanatical. Weekend roads are packed with MAMILs (middle aged men in

Lycra) pedalling expensive racers as fast as they can. The numbers entering the marathons are growing every year. The world seems to be dividing into people who don't exercise and people who do it with missionary zeal. You join a tribe with its own jargon, uniform, kit and social circle. It is all highly organised in a way that our parents' generation would have found bewildering.

The twenty six Bikram postures, bookended by two breathing exercises, are controversial in the yoga world. The originator is the Beverley Hills based multi millionaire Bikram Choudhury. After growing up in India he came to the US in the 1970s. His approach to his branded series of yoga postures is big and bombastic. He has sued yoga studios, claiming ownership of the methods. According to one of the legends that has grown up around his success, Shirley MacLaine told Bikram in the 1970s that he should charge for his yoga because this was the American way.

Studios like Anne Leonard's don't pay him a licence fee but they must comply with key rules: the heat, mirrors on two walls and a carpeted floor. To set up a Bikram studio, teachers have to do a nine week course in the US which currently costs more than ten thousand dollars per person.

Each class follows a similar script (they call it a dialogue) that talks people through the postures in the same sequence each time. Each posture except the final one is performed twice. For many yoga practitioners Bikram is the McYoga of this ancient eastern discipline. Like a Big Mac you will get the same experience at every class in every corner of the world. In Athlone or Athens you will be told to stand with your 'toes touching skin to skin'. You will be asked to open your chest 'like a flower petal blooming'.

Anne Leonard had just welcomed William, a visiting teacher from the US. The laconic American taught a brilliant class, his voice like Garrison Keillor, his approach full of life experience and wry asides. He started the yoga when he was fifty seven. 'Now he's sixty two,' Leonard explains. 'And he came off a transatlantic flight looking like a spring chicken. A lot of the yoga teachers in the US are young, lithe and perfectly tattooed. He's a breath of fresh air because it's real life here. He's in his sixties and he's off all medication [for age related conditions like high blood pressure].'

In America the Bikram studios empty in summer but Anne Leonard's studio had their second busiest month in August 2011, second after January when people rise out of the post Christmas slump and start classes. 'After a bank holiday, any time people have room for contemplation in their lives, we get busier,' Leonard says. 'During the recession we got busier because people have more time to see what they need to do in their lives.'

When I started doing Bikram for the second time, two months after my third son was born, I found it brought mental benefits along with the physical ones. I would leave the house vibrating with tension and tiredness and come home, still tired, but with the frustrations of the day sweated out. At the end of the class, as I lay on the floor, feeling my sweat run off me on to the towel, an idea for a piece of work or a solution to a problem would pop into my head. But I had to factor in the endorphin rush. Post Bikram ideas were a little like drunken ones. They seemed brilliant and glittering but not all of them stood up to scrutiny once the happy haze had worn off.

Now the studio was preparing for a thirty day challenge. This would involve a ninety minute class every day for thirty days. It was a big challenge, to bend my daily life around visits to this warehouse in an industrial estate where the studio was located, having moved from the original lock up. It would be a two hour chunk of time out of my day, every day, seven days a week.

I had only ever done three or four yoga classes in a row, going every day after a break to get back into the rhythm and get used to the heat again. It was now or never. After almost eight years of juggling work and motherhood I had something approaching full time childcare. Liam would be minding the boys when I was at most of the yoga classes. We had just come out of the second of two frozen winters and Dublin was having a technicolour spring: everything bursting with blossom and colour. There wasn't going to be a better time to start.

'When you lose yourself [in the mirror] grab your heels.'

It's easy to tell a weekend class from a weekday one. People arrive more relaxed. During the week you can see their tension rising like steam as they prepare for class, the hassled phone conversations in the changing room, the frustrations and stresses of the day's work visible in their faces. Then they step away from that into the class. It's as far from watching TV on a gym treadmill as you can get. There is a stern simplicity in shedding the work clothes, picking up a towel, mat and water and climbing the stairs to the hot room. There is nothing else to do for the next ninety minutes. There is no noise other than the voice of the teacher and the breathing of the class.

The floor to ceiling mirrors in a Bikram studio feel strange. At first it's difficult to meet your own gaze in a mirror and concentrate on lining up your limbs as closely as you can to the instructions. A strict caste system of competence exists in the class with more experienced people standing in the row in front of the mirrors and the newer people behind them. When I got the nerve to stand in the front row I preferred it there. Having people in front of me and behind me made me feel more claustrophobic.

Day one of the thirty days was daunting. It felt like a first class, although I had been doing Bikram for a while. The unhelpful voice in my head was saying, 'One down, twenty nine to go.' But thoughts were always more pessimistic at the start of class. The first posture, half moon pose, was and still is the one I hate most. It sounds gentle. You stand with your arms raised over your head, almost like a diver waiting to plunge. Your fingers are clasped with the index fingers pointing up, as if firing an imaginary pistol. Then you tilt sideways from the hips to form a crescent shape, the tips of your fingers and the tips of your toes forming the tips of the crescent. It's difficult to do it without twisting your waist and pulling your hips and shoulders out of line. Some of the more flexible hinge at the hips almost to a right angle, like a blade of grass bending in the wind. I was more brittle twig than blade of grass. It's a posture that feels as if it lasts for ever.

Life was getting busy outside the studio that week. My to do list included the simple task: 'buy calendar and red marker'. I had a plan to mark off the days, one to thirty, on a large wall calendar, giving myself a little moment of achievement each day as I counted them off in big red numerals. I never got around to buying the calendar.

Instead, I got to seven classes in a row, marking them off in a diary, then I took a Sunday off. The next day was Monday and I faced into 'the double' as it's known. A double class, back to back, three hours of Bikram yoga with a half hour break between the two classes.

'I can do it,' the small girl shouted as she pedalled her bright green bike along the street, just out of reach of her mother's hand, which hovered near the back of the saddle. 'Yes. You can do it,' I heard her mother say. 'But mind the tree…'

It was in that 'Look, I can do it' spirit of childhood delight in learning something new that I was cycling by on my way to attempt a double Bikram class.

I was dreading it. 'Should I leave the studio between classes?' I asked Lucy, one of the teachers. 'Whatever you feel like doing,' she said. I could shower, change, put down a fresh towel or just take a half hour savasana, or corpse pose, lying there waiting for the second class to start.

The minutes before the first class started were tough. I wondered if I would feel sick, get a headache and have to leave the room. Would my muscles just cramp or shake in protest. As I started the first breathing exercise my neck joints complained painfully. Half moon was the usual torture. In the forward bending part my head felt as if it was filling with fluid, like one of those 1970s dipping bird toys. My sinuses and ears felt blocked, almost blocking out the voice of the teacher.

I felt we were being made to stay in the half moon posture a long time, as the teacher corrected people by name, each correction adding another few seconds to my discomfort. I waited to hear her voice rise on the last 'Push', which usually happens before she utters the blessed words, 'And release.'

The minutes after I straightened and got a familiar light headed rush were the most challenging. I was going to have to do this again, then twice more in a second class.

But (and this was what keeps bringing me back to the Bikram studio to breathe the soupy, sweaty air) the second set was easier. My spine seemed to be loosening up. After that first dreadful posture was over I got into my stride. My knee was still maddeningly far away from my head when I tried to bend over and get the two to meet during standing head to knee. This is fiendishly difficult and followed by the even more difficult standing bow. You grab hold of one foot from behind and bend forward, stretching the fingertips of the other hand towards the mirror. The hardcore Bikram crew (Bikram black belts, as one friend joked) can stretch their top leg straight up to the ceiling, doing standing splits with the forward arm like an arrow pointing straight to the front. The rest of us look like drunken rocking horses, tipping forward, falling out of the posture during the sixty seconds we are supposed to hold it. I fell out several times during that first class of the double but I was gratified to see more of my foot above the top of my head and feel my spine bowing.

By the time we got to triangle pose I began to think I might be able for this. Sweat was running in rivulets down from my scalp and over my collarbones and soaking into the towel under my feet. I glanced at the man next to me: his towel was black with a chalk outline of a dead body from a crime scene. It seemed grimly apt. Then we lay down for the floor exercises and I knew I could get to the end of the first class.

It was strange staying there when the lights came on and almost everyone from my first class left the room. Fresh, cool air came in from the open door beside me. I put down a clean towel and drank a coconut water (which tasted vile, like something squeezed out of a surfer's shorts). My clothes started to feel cold on me, like still wet togs on a beach after your skin has dried. The sweat had dried on my skin and my hair was channelling Albert Einstein. I patted it down and tried to make it less scary. As the people for the next class started to come in I was struck by the fresh smells that everyone carried, different synthetic fragrances of florals and mint, limey scents of perfume, aftershave and deodorant. By the end of this second class all these individuals would have the same generic Bikram stink as me, the salty sweat of forty or fifty strangers oozing from our pores and soaking into our towels and gear.

It was nice to have a sea of new, fresh faces around me. It was even nicer to see behind me Aileen Denvir, who was also staying for a second class. I found out later that she travels up from County Kildare to take Bikram so it makes sense to stay on for a second class rather than making the journey twice. A mother of four, she runs a guest house near Naas and started doing Bikram in September 2010 when a friend recommended it. She was fit, a regular gym goer and tennis player. After the third class she began to see that this was going to work for her, a tall woman with lower back stiffness.

How does she fit it in? 'I think you make time. People say they can't do things because they don't have time but you organise yourself beforehand and you make time.'

Later that year she took a flight to LA and checked into a room in the Radisson Airport Hotel at LAX for the nine weeks of Bikram teacher training. In the ballroom where classes are held, hundreds of people from twenty six countries are packed in like sweaty sardines, foot to face, several rows deep. She believes there were seven hundred people in one class. The nine week course costs $10,200, not including food. It was intense, an enormous challenge, a yoga bubble out of which she emerged feeling glad she had done it.

Right now, back in the class where I was doing my first double, I was starting to feel calmer and more optimistic. The endorphin rush from the first class had kicked in. I was still worried that my muscles would fail me but I looked in the mirror and felt peaceful. Nothing to do now but the next ninety minute class. I was in the zone.

During the breathing exercise I inhaled and exhaled deeply and without the impatience I often feel to get to the end of this preamble. I've tried counting the breaths each teacher gives but usually give up around ten. Sometimes it seems to be ten, sometimes more.

Half moon pose felt slightly easier this time. My muscles were aching with fatigue. During the poses in which I was standing on one leg I felt muscles tremble but my focus was stronger than I was used to and this seemed to keep me in the postures as long as I needed. It was immensely satisfying to lie down on the floor at the end of the standing series.

After each floor posture I could feel the ache of tiredness in my muscles. My heart seemed be beating out of my chest during each *savasana*, also known as corpse pose, which involves lying as still as possible and letting your pounding heart return to a normal rate. By now it was hard to think of anything other than this room and the next posture. By the end of the second class my thumb and forefinger felt sticky to the touch as I lay on the floor. I realised I wasn't as thirsty as I would normally be at this stage in a class. Maybe it was the coconut water or maybe I had lost less fluid.

The teacher, Fiona, talked about the idea of doing this yoga every day for a thirty day challenge. Doing it would result in a new body and a new mind, she said, and it would take our yoga practice to a new level.

When I sat up my hands felt smooth and swollen, as if I had sweated off my fingerprints. My skin was flushed red and blotchy. The sweat was drying quickly again and I felt cold, hungry, tired and happy. The short cycle home on a beautiful spring evening was trippy. The leaves on the canal trees looked silky, like green skin. The light of dusk on the mirror of canal water was glorious. The air flowed over me, reminding me of that sensation of swimming through watery air that I felt after my first Bikram classes. I was a bird on a thermal, freewheeling down a hill on my bike. I could smell things growing, the occasional whiff of smoke from someone's fireplace on the still cool night. I passed by the taxi man who lives on our road and polishes his car almost every day. He was sitting in the gleaming black car, like a grand piano on wheels. We exchanged waves.

I once mentioned this post Bikram feeling to a friend who tried out a few classes. It's great once you get out, she agreed, adding drily that the inmates of Guantanamo probably feel the same way on their release.

At home I was shaky with hunger and wolfed down a plate of spaghetti Bolognese with about twice the pasta I would normally eat. Liam's laptop was on the table. Normally I would itch to lift the lid and check my email or Twitter account as I ate my dinner. I didn't feel any desire to do that. Instead I read a newspaper and the laptop was pushed out of the way. My eldest son was reading Harry Potter, buried in an armchair beside me. We sat and read in companionable silence. 'How was your yoga class, Mum?' he asked eventually.

'It was hard but I did it,' I said. 'I did it all twice.'

'At least you didn't have to do a second class that was different' – this with all the logic of an eight year old.

The next class (by now I was at class ten) felt like a walk in the park. It was the payoff for the double, pushing myself past where I was sure I could go and managing it. The yoga had become a routine, still difficult but less difficult than ten days earlier. The heat wasn't as much of a challenge. I had a rhythm and a method. I could get up from my desk at home, locate and pack two towels – one to sweat on, another to dry off after a shower – my gear and a bottle of water in seconds and cycle to the studio in just over five minutes. The smell of the Bikram studio began to creep into the house, the sweat rising off my gear in the laundry basket. The washing machine churned and gurgled almost constantly. I blessed a breezy day when I could hang the towels on the line and take them off fresh and dry before class.

Then came day fourteen, 'the hangover class'. I was at the midway point and let myself relax a little too much at a Good Friday night pot luck supper in a friend's house. Cycling home in the early hours of the morning of Easter Saturday was like travelling through a film set or a post apocalyptic city, as Good Friday is the one night of the year that pubs and clubs are closed. At Bikram the next morning I spent the first hour of class in a bubble of nausea and unease. By the end of the class I felt I was sweating alcohol into the towel.

Easter Sunday provided a break as there was no class. At the 10am class on Easter Monday every member of the studio seemed to be there, with four rows and just a few inches between towels. I went back to do a second class at 6.30pm that day. It was my sixteenth class and something clicked that evening. I felt flexible and strong, able to do this without a huge struggle.

Later, when I sat in the office of sports psychologist Catherine Woods in Dublin City University, she said something that made sense of this phase when things began to work, just after the halfway point in my thirty days. Look at a small child trying to learn to use a scooter or ride a bike, she said. The child is dogged and focused, undeterred by the number of times he or she falls off. They can't scoot very quickly or with much direction. 'It's learning based on mastering as opposed to performance, learning and being better than you were the last time you did it.'

Small children set themselves up as their own project. They are not put off by the fact that they are terrible at something when they first attempt it. They work at it until they get better. Between the ages of six and twelve, Woods explained, they start comparing their performance to other children, moving from the mastery to the ego stage. During the mastery stage the joy is in the learning, the grin of achievement at a first scoot or pedal or climbing the slide. Then they go through the ego stage, exposed to the idea of being better or worse than everybody else. A solid sense of self will bring children back to an idea of mastery as a worthwhile exercise and of using their failures as opportunities to improve. 'Mastery ties completely into intrinsic motivation, because you are now matching your ability to the challenge that you undertake. Once challenge meets ability you get a sense of flow.'

There is plenty in the Bikram monologue about not comparing yourself to anyone else. 'Focus on your own eyes in the mirror,' you are told. But Bikram devotees are a competitive lot. And that shedding of ego (comparing your performance to another person's bow pulling posture or standing head to knee) and trying to concentrate on your own ability to do something can be as challenging as the heat or the postures. The best classes were the ones when I barely glanced at the people around me. I became a Bikram robot, staring straight ahead at my face as it grew pink and shiny with sweat, resisting the urge to fix my hair or adjust my clothes. At these classes I was able to listen better, learn more and do more, tuning into where my muscles were and how I was using them.

Doing a class every day became part of my day. I hadn't flopped down on the couch for weeks. Television was no longer an option. I was either going to an evening class or collapsing into bed, exhausted and craving sleep.

Carving out the time wasn't without its difficulties. One Saturday afternoon I dropped my middle son at a birthday party on the way to class. The party was due to end before I finished class but I had forgotten to give Liam the address of the party house so he could pick him up. I had to jump up and run out of the Bikram class to ring him. I had guilty visions of my four year old standing with his party bag, forlorn in the aftermath of the birthday and wondering where we were. It was at times like this that the whole idea of trying to fit a thirty day challenge into family life seemed to be pushing the limits of the possible.

I spoke to other people who had 'done the challenge' the year before. One woman talked about finding it 'oppressive', that obligation to do a class every day, to bend your life around something so demanding. My motivation started to sag a little around the twentieth class. Ten more classes seemed like a huge task and I began to feel the pace of the previous three weeks. Tiredness was beginning to be a problem.

The day after my twenty seventh class I sat with friends in a hotel in Cork and forgot to keep track of the number of glasses of wine I was drinking. Twenty seven Bikram classes had turned every molecule of my body into a sponge for alcohol. The next morning I felt so ill I had to lie on the bed with a cold washcloth on my face for a couple of hours before I could face the journey home.

Day thirty was marked by a double class to finish off. I reeled out of the studio at 10.30 on the evening of 9 May. Summer was coming to Dublin and I had done it. During the thirty days I had slept brilliantly, worked hard and felt a little more patient with my children. I had improved my flexibility and balance. I still couldn't do every posture perfectly but I was a little closer than I had been at the start. The most profound difference was in my head rather than in my body. Doing something as difficult as this had made life outside the yoga studio seem easier. I came away from each class feeling a sense of peace.

Thirty days of Bikram is not for everyone but the yoga world is wide and full of different kinds of practice to suit different people. The need for the kind of movement and stretching involved in yoga has never been greater. Increasingly we spend our time bending over small fiddly things. We peer at texts or tap an email into the tiny backlit screen of a smartphone. We crunch our necks and spines and all the muscles around them. My husband's sister in law (a sports and rehabilitation physiotherapist) finally got to the bottom of my neck stiffness when she asked whether I spent a long time working on a laptop. I did. Without a remote keyboard and mouse I was giving myself neck problems by looking down at the screen. The machine was at desktop level to allow me to type. If I raised the screen I had to hold my arms in the air to use the keyboard. There is no physically comfortable way to work on a laptop for extended periods of time.

In most yoga classes you will do some form of backward bend. This is a range of motion that we lose in modern western life. We drive, work, eat and now increasingly watch television with hunched shoulders. Pushing our shoulders back and down and stretching our necks up and back is a movement many people do only in a yoga session. It's a posture that is challenging. You can feel dizzy or sick if you look up and back. But the more I did it the better my back and neck felt.

At a certain point in life you start getting worse at things. Your eyesight slides slowly to the stage where you have to extend a menu or a book out the full length of your arm to see things. Your joints stiffen and, as the old Billy Connolly sketch goes, you start to make that spontaneous groaning sound when you bend down to pick something up. Doing thirty days of yoga had allowed me to start getting better at something, not dramatically but subtly. I could feel even my forty year old muscles strengthening marginally. My balance improved. I could concentrate a little better.

The bigger surprise was the mental benefit of doing a class every day for thirty days. At each class something untangled itself in my thinking, whether it was the opening paragraph of a restaurant review I was working on, an idea for a piece or a solution to some time juggling challenge in the days ahead. Given the time and space and silence of a class during the resting stages I was able to think more clearly. On the smelly island of Bikram I could haul myself out of a churning sea and think straight. At other times of the day I could have one, two or three children talking to me and a dog pawing at my leg, asking for something. Now mine was the only voice and by the end of each class that inner voice was a more positive one. The bleaker thoughts had gone, dripped on to the floor along with a lot of sweat.

At the end of one class I turned and lay resting, feeling my heart pounding into the floor. Other people lay silently around me and the heartbeat I could feel in my chest was like a shared heartbeat. It was as if the rhythm was coming not from me but from the floor, generated by this group of strangers who had just done more or less the same physically demanding things I had done.

I knew I wasn't the kind of person who wanted to continue doing a Bikram class every day. One of the joys of doing it for thirty days was the joy of stopping. Now that summer had come I was longing to be outside, under a big open sky, instead of in a strip lit carpeted room, watching the sweat run down my face like tears.

An Evening with the Guru

It's the shoes that kill me. Dressed in a shiny grey suit, which he proudly declares to be his gangster look, Bikram Choudhury is pacing around a small stage in the Astra Hall of UCD. On his feet are a pair of chunky heeled court shoes, grey patent, with bows on top. The glittery hem of his pimp suit brushes them as he walks and talks, for hours, without a script.

This is a man who likes to play with his audience and their preconceived idea of a guru. He tells us he wants to look like 'a yogi from Beverley Hills'. His long black hair is pushed back with a microphone headset and springs out wildly behind him. It is an astonishing presentation, full of breathtaking claims, bravado, one liners and anecdotes. Anyone hoping to get a few hints on how to improve their flexibility or tackle a tricky posture has come to the wrong lecture.

Bounding on to the small platform stage he scorns the large

comfy chair decorated with an orange throw – 'I'm not handicapped yet' – and sips disgustedly at the cup of something hot, ignoring the bottle of full sugar Coke. This is not going to be a serene fireside chat. It's the all moving all talking Bikram show. Amsterdam, Madrid, Ibiza have already been clocked up. He asks jokingly where he is now. It has more than a touch of the rock star's 'Hello... Dublin.'

'I sell the highest selling product of the world of all time,' he declares, with his trademark bombast. He has, he says, seven billion customers and his business has increased by 65 per cent. That product is 'life,' he says, 'not in a wheelchair, or jail, not broke or in a mental hospital.' He is selling Indian culture and he's doing it Las Vegas style.

There are words of something that sounds like wisdom. 'Life is more simple, more clean, more straight than a piece of crystal. But we, idiots, we make life so complicated. We live in a booby trap.'

Then he talks about selling people the chance to live to a hundred, to be disco dancing with their great grandchildren at their one hundredth birthday. It's a beguiling promise. To him spirituality means 'building a bridge between your spirit and your mind'. And for him Bikram yoga is the idea that 'with the body we can totally control the mind'. We westerners have 'a junk body, a screw loose brain and a lost soul,' he insists at one point, adding the punch line: 'Good luck with your life.'

He talks about his fast cars and tells a story about how he owns 'the biggest swimming pool in Beverley Hills' but doesn't know how to swim. There is a story about being flown from Tokyo to Honolulu in 1974 to treat Richard Nixon and being rewarded with an American green card. It's the Bikram schtick and it's a familiar script, unhindered by modesty or self deprecation.

Yet there are moments, like nuggets of truth in a box of tinsel, that resonate with me: 'My job is to make you see who you are,' he says at one point. It's also about making practitioners see with their 'third eye', their positive happy eye that sees the world for the beautiful place it is. This rings true to my experience of that post Bikram bliss.

Then it's back to the car salesman talk. 'I'm a businessman,' he says, tapping his shining head with a slim index finger. 'I make everybody happy.' At one point he tries to tell the time on his watch. 'Too much diamonds. I can't see it,' he complains.

The bizarre presentation from this guru, more Elvis than Messiah, has worked in a way. Instead of wanting to touch the hem of his shiny trousers he leaves his audience wanting to touch their own toes. We are the gods, he tells us. His bling and bombast are a Teflon coating to repel any guru worship. So he throws the challenge back to us to bend, stretch and breathe our way to a state of peace.

4

Motivation Comes from Doing

'Nice new shoes, Mum,' my four year old son said, catching sight of my whiter than white trainers. His older brother chimed in with a similar compliment. But the trainers are not new. I've had them for years. They're new to my sons, who have no memory of seeing me wearing them before. Coupled with the fact that I almost couldn't find jogging pants this morning, I was starting this next thirty day challenge from a low base.

If I'm looking for something other than me to blame for my lack of sportiness I might start with my convent school education. If you started out sporty you could survive the PE regime in the average 1980s girls' secondary school. But if, like me, you were a bit ambivalent about running, then there was plenty to put you off. It started with the sports uniform, a white Aertex top (usually grey from washing by week three of term) and a pair of claret coloured culottes, just the colour to set off pale, goose fleshed Irish legs. The culottes were heavy polyester with a low slung crotch, not so much a garment as an anti running device. I remember one annual cross country run which consisted of bringing a couple of hundred teenage girls up the steepest hill out of the town, round by a top field and back again. The smokers hung back and took sneaky drags, ready to fling the butts into the hedgerows at the sight of a teacher, while the keener runners charged ahead. I was somewhere in the middle.

That morning I was on my way to Dublin City University's School of Health and Human Performance. I was to run on a treadmill in a lab to see how fit I was before I started a thirty day aerobic fitness challenge. The idea was to do something aerobically challenging every day and see what I could achieve. Sports scientists were going to assess me down to the particles in my blood to see what, if any, improvement a daily regime of aerobic exercise could bring. I was interested to see whether I could get fitter, improve at something rather than just give in to the general slide. I am at an age where you begin to get used to getting worse at things rather than better. Sometimes my knees creak more loudly than the stairs when I go down for breakfast in the morning.

The vow to get fitter is a common one. It normally happens in a lull or a break from the routine. It might be New Year's Eve or the last night of a holiday. We've all resolved to make more effort, change our physical habits, lose weight, get fit, give up smoking or drinking or eating the wrong kinds of foods. We often make these plans in a place removed from everyday life when change seems more possible.

And then there's failure, the slide back into inactivity or the behaviour we wanted to change. It's a familiar pattern, ending with a warm, welcoming hug from our old selves back into our old ways. Until the next time.

I'm interested in the psychology of exercise and fascinated by the cycle of self improvement that happens at various times of the year – the January blitz, the September resolutions – why we feel compelled to do it and why we fall away from it as predictably as we embrace it.

Catherine Woods, Head of the School of Health and Human Performance in Dublin City University, is an expert in those things that trip us up on the path of good intentions. One of the most cited statistics is that within six months of taking up a physical activity one in two of us will have dropped it again. Why?

'Change is not continuous. It doesn't start and continue exponentially. It can go through dips and troughs, depending on your personal or social circumstances,' Dr Woods explains.

My social circumstances of local school drop offs and pick ups helped to get me a basic level of daily activity. Cycling, walking and yoga had kept me pretty fit but I realised shortly after I got on to the large grey treadmill in the DCU sports lab that I could barely run to save my life.

The School of Health and Human Performance feels like a mixture of gym and hospital: long clean corridors with labs off them in the basement of one of the campus buildings. The staff see two main groups of people – elite athletes (sports people interested in honing their training regime) and people who have had cardiac episodes and are now using fitness to keep themselves healthy. The scientists who run the school believe firmly in exercise as a preventative medicine, something that everyone, from nursery to nursing home, needs to incorporate into their daily routine.

The first test was an ultrasound of one of my arteries to assess how strongly my blood vessels were able to pump blood around my body. Part of the test was a nitroglycerine spritz under the tongue to open the arteries completely. Typically used as the first treatment after a cardiac arrest, the spray tasted like a super strong mouthwash and made me feel a bit light headed and woozy. On the screen beside me I could see the walls of the artery changing from wobbly lines into a series of straight lines, like a barcode, in response to the chemicals.

Next I was weighed and measured. At 60.5 kilos I have a BMI of twenty one, which is good. Then some samples of blood were taken for lecturer Ronan Murphy to test for micro particles. These micro particles, or cells, would be shed by my vascular system into my blood stream in response to the stress of exercise. The level of cells, particularly endothelial cells, was a good indication of my fitness and heart health. The number of particles my system would shed and the rate at which my levels returned to normal would provide an extremely accurate test of fitness.

Then in one of these artificially lit rooms I took my toughest test, pounding on a treadmill for four minute periods at ever increasing speed, with a mouthpiece gripped in my teeth so a computer could assess my lung capacity. I felt awkward and leaden on the treadmill, my legs getting heavier by the minute. I felt as if I were gasping for air and never reached a rhythm that felt sustainable. Occasionally I would stop running to have a tiny blood sample taken from my ear to assess lactate levels in my blood. My mouth was dry and I had a claustrophobic feeling of being unable to swallow. For the final test I had to run without stopping for as long as I could, as the gradient was steadily increased. My lungs felt as if they were going to explode. By the time I put up my hand to stop it all, a niggling pain had started in my left knee as a little reminder of why I'd given up running before.

Dr Woods cites five stages of change that people go through before successfully putting daily exercise into their lives. The first stage, which seems more like a pre stage, is the 'no behaviour and no intention' one. It's the deepest trough out of which it can seem impossible to climb, when the person is not doing any form of physical activity and has no intention of getting active in the next thirty days. 'It's not on their radar. It's not a priority for them. That could be because of work issues or anything, really. For that person to change, the first thing they have to do is realise the health consequences of inactivity,' says Dr Woods, 'and the health benefits to them [of activity] and that's the important thing.'

The second stage is when there is still no behaviour but there is an intention. 'Now they're thinking about it, considering joining a class or walking to work. Then they need to decide, "This is something I want to do. I know there are different types of activity that I can do. I'm going to start on such a day and the pros outweigh the cons." The key thing is reducing the barriers,' she says. This means that if that last minute piece of work keeps you from getting to your 6pm exercise class you plan to take a later class rather than shelving the plan to take exercise.

Stage three is preparation. 'The person is becoming engaged in physical activity but not every day. They're not meeting the thirty minute criteria. These would be the weekend warriors, infrequent exercisers. But the intention is firmly there and they have moved from thinking about something to actually doing it. That is massive.'

And it is at this third stage that many people find things challenging. I've probably been in that third stage with several types of exercise in the past. That third stage is the reason for the abandoned sports equipment in our lives, the dusty cross trainer that's now used as a clothes horse, the forlorn tennis racquet at the back of the under stairs cupboard. 'If you do that before you're ready or in a ill prepared way you're setting yourself up for failure,' Dr Woods says. 'How have you prepared a path to prioritise it? Is there someone else to look after the kids so that time is now prioritised?'

For setting fitness goals, Woods cites the acronym SMARTER, standing for Specific Measurable Agreed Realistic Time bound Enjoyable and Recorded goals. It's important, she says, to 'physically write them down somewhere and ideally put that somewhere public so you're really saying, "Right, this is me really thinking about something." You're not back at contemplation.'

And what does she make of the idea of doing something every day for thirty days? 'That's a really good idea. What we're trying to get across is it doesn't matter whether it's five minutes a day or fifty minutes a day. A little bit frequently leads to a habit. Start it in May or June when the weather is supposed to be good. Hopefully it's building a pattern of good behaviour. Make sure you've thought about it, prepared a path, planned your goals, been realistic; then pat yourself on the back when you've actually achieved something.'

The fourth stage of change is when you are meeting the criteria of thirty minutes a day at least five days a week 'and it's really bedding down,' but, Dr Woods warns, 'this is where the risk of relapse becomes a challenge.' Confidence can dip. Circumstances can change, with a holiday or a change of job.

At this stage the enjoyment factor is a huge decider of whether or not the new activity will stick. If it's something you enjoy you will be intrinsically motivated. You'll be doing it because it gives you pleasure rather than as a slog or a duty. It becomes part of who you are, knitted into the fabric of your life. You will feel out of sorts if you haven't exercised.

The final stage is maintenance, when you've been doing daily physical activity for six months and it's really solid behaviour and the likelihood of relapse is much less. 'We find roughly 25 per cent of our adult population would be in that maintenance phase. But roughly 75 per cent are struggling and are somewhere in the first four stages. Almost two thirds are in the first three.'

There are external factors that can help us, Dr Woods believes, like the design of our cities and towns. Transport policies that provide safe walking and cycling areas and schools that encourage children to be physically active as part of their education all help.

How we think about our physical performance is also intrinsic to success. In a way we should be going back to the stage of a small child, Woods explains. If we can base our expectations on mastering a skill rather than trying to compete with others it becomes much more satisfying.

This harks back to how I began to feel about the intensive yoga class when I forgot about comparing myself to everyone else in the room and concentrated on learning. A small child uses this mastery stage to learn basic skills – how to use a scooter or ride a bike.

'Mastery ties completely into intrinsic motivation,' Dr Woods says, 'because you are now matching your ability to the challenge you undertake. Once challenge meets ability you get a sense of flow.'

As parents we can show our children an example of how to be active every day. According to DCU's research the need to change our children's exercise habits is becoming urgent. In a recent study of five thousand children only 14 per cent of them were meeting the criteria for physical activity. 'Eighty six per cent were insufficiently active.'

The stages of change are not linear: planning before you start will help the new regime stick. 'It has to work with your lifestyle. It has to be easy. A lot of time for myself cycling in and out to work is how I get my exercise. It works. So even on days when I don't get to the gym or out for a run at least I've got that type of activity in my lifestyle.'

If you're not doing anything minutes count.

Dr Woods's colleague, sports psychologist Siobhan McArdle, is also interested in the idea of motivation, that impulse that makes people make time for exercise. 'Many people say they don't feel like doing it so they have to wait until they feel like doing it. But we know that doing fosters motivation. So you don't wait. You do. As a result of doing it you feel greater motivation, then you do it again.'

It's simple. Motivation comes from doing. So my plan to do something every day would fit with that idea. I simply had to do it, whatever the weather or my mood or energy levels.

People can also suffer by failing to plan what it is they want to do. They try to do too much too quickly so they feel inadequate, McArdle explains. 'So they don't enjoy what they're doing. So really thinking through the programme and how you approach it is critical. Find something you're going to be able to enjoy.'

Her area of interest is in the use of exercise as a treatment for depression. 'Certainly we know that changes in cognition stem quite a bit from changes in emotion. So when you engage in exercise it makes you feel a certain way and that feeling can influence a change in cognition which has a knock on effect for mood and depression.'

'The WHO has warned that depression will be the second biggest worldwide health concern after cardiovascular disease by 2020,' McArdle says. 'So research into exercise as medicine for depression is beginning to target this area.'

There are no set guidelines on how much or how often exercise should be used. McArdle explains. 'In terms of our clinical guidelines for the treatment of depression the number one intervention is CBT and, within that, the first strategy they use is activation. So you get the person moving. It comes from that branch of psychology. Do first and that will have implications for the way you feel. It'll change your motivation and change the way you feel and the way you think.'

The GP who would recommend exercise as a treatment for depression is probably the exception to the rule; antidepressants, which can lead to weight gain, are a common treatment.

Exercise is believed to have a positive effect on mood, not only because of the physical payoff but because it is a distraction from the constantly worrying mind. 'For the forty minutes or twenty minutes that you're exercising you're not worrying and that may reduce anxiety.'

As I clamber off the treadmill I wonder whether I can do thirty days of running in any form. It's necessary because running is going to do more for me than cycling, research technician Paul O'Connor explained. It will burn more energy and increase my aerobic fitness more effectively because it's more difficult. So I have to run.

'Right,' I joked to Paul as I clambered down off the treadmill. 'I'm off to do what everyone does when they start a fitness programme: I'm going to buy new stuff.' I asked him what kind of trainers I should buy. He said that one of his colleagues was researching the science of barefoot running and now spends his day padding around the corridors barefoot. 'Youtube Daniel Lieberman,' he said.

Suddenly I was in a whole other realm of thinking about running. Lieberman is a Harvard professor whose speciality is the biology of human evolution. He believes the human physique, or how our bodies are built, is a result of how we evolved to run, to hunt down prey. Effective humans were the ones who could catch their dinner by running it to the point of exhaustion.

Video clips show Lieberman explaining the physiology of how we run differently in running shoes. He believes the built up cushioned heels help us to run with a heel strike, which is not how we were designed to run. In a study of Kenyan runners who had never worn shoes he found that none of them were hitting the ground with their heels. They ran with a forefoot strike. At the end of the clip you see Lieberman running barefoot on the pavements in a snowy American city.

I was intrigued. My second source of information was Jason Robillard, a keen runner who had suffered many injuries and become an advocate and teacher of barefoot running. His book was available to download free from the Internet.

My final expert opinion came from exercise physiologist Professor Niall Moyna, who became more famous outside the corridors of DCU recently, thanks to his association with the Dublin Gaelic football team and their success in the 2011 All Ireland. He is fascinated by the fact that exercise and diet work differently for different people. After a stint in the US working on exercise as preventative medicine he is also driven by a desire to improve the health of our teenage population.

Ultrasounds and blood tests carried out on the vascular system of overweight teenagers have shown that they will be at risk of a heart attack in their twenties. 'The heart is one of the few muscles that doesn't regenerate. That's what's coming down the road for us.'

His single 'magic bullet' would be to give teenagers an incentive to maintain their aerobic fitness. 'I'd give every kid in Ireland a thousand euros if they were aerobically fit by the time they got to Leaving Cert.' A simple goal of aerobic fitness would eliminate weight, diabetes and other chronic health problems.

And what about the idea of getting fitter by doing something every day? 'I believe it's not about getting people fit; it's about changing behaviour in a way that can be maintained. When it comes to health and lifestyle it's about adopting healthy behaviours. If someone asks me what they should do I'd say, "Five minutes a day every day of the week, that's thirty five minutes a week or 150 a month; that's around 1500 minutes a year. That's better than no minutes. Then every second day do six minutes. Then figure out the average amount of exercise you can easily fit into your lifestyle." It's not rocket science to go out and walk. 90 per cent of the population could initiate a walking programme without seeing their primary care physician.

'You don't have to do it in one bout. You can accumulate that thirty minutes over the course of a day. Break it into smaller amounts. We have to come up with prescriptions that make it easier for people to adopt healthy behaviour.'

The key is the individual finding what works for them, then absorbing it into their daily life, Dr Moyna believes. 'What works for you may not work for everybody. We're all a little bit different. From a public health perspective we have to get people undertaking lifestyle activities that can be sustained.'

A few days later I was packing my case for our summer holiday in France and the trainers were staying at home. The 'Uh oh, here we go again' look passed briefly over my husband's face as I explained that I was going to run barefoot for thirty days. Other people reacted as if I had told them I was going to run naked. I could do it with minimalist shoes – light pool type shoes with separate articulated toes, like gloves for feet. But as they were available only from specialist online suppliers I couldn't find a pair in time for our trip. So I was taking the extreme first step of leaving my running shoes at home. I bought discount supermarket running gear (probably the ugliest clothing I've ever owned) and a heart rate monitor which refused to let me be born any earlier than 1980 when I tried to set it. Despite all the misgivings I was going to try this. A sense of freedom with nothing more than a few blisters and no knee or hip problems awaited me. Or so I hoped.

Day One

My calves are burning and the soles of my feet are tingling and smarting as if they've been repeatedly slapped. I have a couple of faint bruises on my soles but my first toe dip into barefoot running has been OK. I can't face the gravel strewn tarmac roads around the house where we're staying in Normandy. In cushioned trainers it's a nice running route with a few gentle slopes on the quiet one car width roads, but barefoot it looks like it would be a path of pain, Croagh Patrick style. I'm not brave enough to take it on. Instead I head to the nearest beach. Luckily it's Quineville, a beautiful long strand north of the Normandy landing beaches of the Second World War.

Most of the main beach has sharp shells so I pick my way across the surface to a stretch beyond a stream. On the banks of the stream the sand turns to a soupy mud that squelches up between my toes unpleasantly. It's a startling feeling, how I would imagine it feels to stand barefoot in a pool of fresh cow pats.

The tide is out and the sand looks promising. As I pick my way across the shell strewn surface I wonder why I'm doing this. My Fitflops are a couple of hundred feet back. All I have are my feet and my heart monitor with a wristwatch readout. I'm aiming to train at 160 to 165 heartbeats per minute for two minutes, then drop to a fast walk for another two minutes, then run again. The effect is something like a barefoot March hare as I run, looking at my watch, in one direction, then turn and run off back again. At one point a large white dog finds me irresistible and bounds up to join in, until his owner calls him off. I keep it up for forty minutes (two minutes running, two minutes walking) until my calves start to complain. The normally dicky left knee is fine but my calf muscles are not used to this kind of activity and the aches set in. I don't want to be hobbling tomorrow so I give it up.

Beach running feels like the perfect first step in barefoot running, firstly because you don't get any puzzled glances. What can be more normal than running barefoot on a beach? It's also exhilarating, the sense of freedom of running under a beautiful summer sky with the sea out beyond me – although the view might as well not exist, as my eyes are fixed on the ground for hazards. One upturned mussel shell could slice through the sole of my foot and put an instant stop to this. A kind of foot eye coordination is involved in running at any speed when the sand is speckled with hazards. My footprints show clearly that my sole is hitting first, making a deeper indent in the sand. My heel is visible in the footprint, but with no indentation.

By the evening I am hobbling downstairs. I hope I haven't pushed my calves too far on the first outing.

Day Two

I am the stiff legged scarecrow, Aunt Sally, from the old children's TV show *Worzel Gummidge*. Bending my legs is agony. I come down the stairs like someone in need of two knee replacements. Eventually I have to turn and walk down backwards. I have knackered my calf muscles.

When I start to read Jason Robillard's book about barefoot running I realise what a rookie mistake I have just made. They even have an acronym for it in the running world: TMTS. Too Much Too Soon. And my choice of sand as a first surface? Also a disaster. Sand is fine once you've been running for a while on a hard surface, learning to run lightly and gently, to kiss the ground with your bare feet and run soundlessly, like a 'ninja', as Robillard recommends, or fluidly like water flowing over rock. I've been pounding a soft surface with muscles that have spent nearly four decades experiencing motion with sturdy shoes strapped to them.

But I have a thirty day challenge and vials of blood are waiting in

DCU freezers with micro particles in them that I have to improve on. My motivation level is on the floor. I am in pain and tired and the chilly, wet weather is not very promising. But I've committed to this. So I pull out my trusty bike to whizz down the narrow lanes to the sea. I've clocked the journey on the car at a little over 4.5 kilometres. Doing it by bike will give me forty minutes or so aerobic exercise. When I get there I can walk, hobble or trot for twenty minutes.

The cycling is lovely. Damp hedgerow smells of cattle and grass and the warm, sugary butter blast from the local *boulangerie* remind me how much I love being on a bike. I can see from my heart monitor that the advice about needing to run was true. Even on the toughest hill and pelting it I can barely get my heart rate over 150 beats per minute.

When I get to the beach it's too painful to run. I try but give up and cycle back.

Day Three
It's time to leave the heart monitor at home. I'm tired racing myself and staring down every few seconds at the digits on this ugly piece of equipment. I know from my breathing when I'm exercising in some kind of zone. And now that running is off the menu I'm going to take to the sea, so the heart monitor is doubly redundant. The tide is out when I get to Quineville and the only people in the water are some French children learning to windsurf. I carefully leave my cycling gear and bag on the sand, far enough from the incoming tide to be safe. The water is lovely, cold and calm, and I swim happily for around ten minutes before eyeing my stuff nervously. I have already seen the speed of this tide. I wade out just in time to scoop everything I have off the sand where the water has encircled it and is licking hungrily, inches from my clothes.

The calves are still in pain. I go from Aunt Sally to John Wayne throughout the day. It's time to go back to basics. Reading Jason Robillard, I realise that I needed to do some basic exercises to get ready to run barefoot. The first is a walking on the spot drill, thinking about lifting rather than dropping each foot so that the other touches the ground without your brain telling it to. After mastering that for five minutes, you move to a leaping into the air soundlessly (like a cat, Robillard advises). This feels ludicrous: I am reminded of Kato in the Clouseau movies leaping out of cupboards on to a startled Peter Sellers. Then I have to learn to pick up things with my foot, Christy Brown style. It's extremely tricky. My sons take up the challenge. The toes of the four year old are much more dextrous than those of his eight year old brother. At dinner outside that evening I shift footfuls of gravel from one place to another under the table.

Day Four

It's raining. I pull the brakes halfway down the muddy lane from the house, ready to turn back and wait for dry weather. Then the sky lightens and I decide to carry on. It's the kind of day when any break in the rain is going to be brief.

On the beach a French family is zipped into their rain gear, looking balefully at the grey black sea. I feel impossibly white as I strip off for my swim. The mad Irishwoman *en vacances*. This time I've brought my goggles but putting my face in the icy water is a step too far. The dark tint on the goggles makes the water murky and dark. So I give up on that and swim breaststroke along by the shore. I get nowhere fast. I am effectively treading water horizontally. And my heart rate is about as raised as it would be during a leisurely walk to the shops.

On the cycle home it gets so wet I feel like I'm cycling in the shower. I get back ravenous and happy. I would not have forced myself out into the weather like this without having the thirty day challenge in the back of my mind. And my day is all the better for it.

Day Five

I've been following Jason Robillard's programme of walking, leaping on the spot and picking up things with my toes. It's time to attempt a run on a hard surface. My calves are feeling better. I cycle down to Quineville in search of the perfect stretch of tarmac. The best I can find is a small side road beside a campsite. I can hear families in their caravans on the other side of the hedge. I take off my flip flops and am barefoot on the warm tar surface. I start with Robillard's relaxation and walking on the spot routine before setting out on a walk. The idea of focusing on lifting rather than stepping down seems to work. It feels lighter on the rough tarmac. There are a few loose stones but the road is mainly clear. Running makes my soles smart but is not too uncomfortable as I start a quick stepping run. This style of running is completely different, mouse steps as opposed to giant *Chariots of Fire* style strides that you see other runners taking. It feels like running apologetically across the road rather than the long limbed idea we have of distance runners. I potter to the end of my small road and turn around to potter back. I'm trying to take roughly three steps per second to keep my stride short and light. This will also keep my feet under my hips so I'm not over striding.

Stepping on to the grass now feels like stepping on to velvet. It's cool and I can feel the gentle mud underneath the silken sheaths of grass. I can see why running on the hard surface makes sense. It's unforgiving of any pounding. Striking the hard ground with my heel first is as unthinkable as banging my head against it. I am running to minimise impact and friction, feeling my way over this hard surface as gingerly as it's possible to do so. I manage about six minutes, then call it a day. No Too Much Too Soon for me today. When I slide my feet back into my Fitflops it feels like strapping two cool mattresses on to my feet.

In a French hypermarket I buy the cheapest trainers I can find to play tennis with my eight year old on a small municipal court. They feel clumpy and alien, the heel built up, making it difficult to land with the forefoot first. They will be more suitable for cycling but I'm already looking forward to taking them off and trying to extend my barefoot trotting to eight minutes tomorrow. The cycle and short running routine is already burning over 500 calories a session, according to my heart monitor. (But then it thinks I'm twenty eight so maybe it's miscalculating my calorie load). Whatever the exact figure I could eat my own body weight in croissants when I get back to the house.

Day Six

It's fascinating to watch how Isaac, our youngest, uses his feet. He's two and a bit and has had the least time of any of us in shoes. Most of the time he forgets about shoes and wanders around all day in his bare feet. As he goes down the smooth five hundred year old stone steps in the Normandy millhouse he splays his toes in mid air, preparing to find the next step. He's always loved going down steps, insisting on doing it unaided from the moment he could walk. He is still making the connections of distance and impact and balance and can do it best in his bare feet. He is improving his physical intelligence. He doesn't walk with his heels hitting the ground first. He seeks out the information he needs with the wide, front, most padded part of his foot. You can see the beauty of the connections between the soles of our feet and our central nervous system.

During our game of tennis my supermarket trainers get so un-comfortable I slip them off and go barefoot. The dark red parts of the painted tarmac court are several degrees hotter than the grass green painted surrounds. I can't pelt for the ball but I trot barefoot around the court happily for forty minutes.

I picture the pads of a dog's paws when I read about how your feet become like soft leather after a long time barefoot running. Mine are a long way off. Today I run for seven minutes on a quiet stretch of road in front of some houses. The inhabitants look at me strangely. Their dogs bark and bare their teeth. I cycle back with smarting soles and an appetite the size of a Normandy cow and spend the rest of the day ruminating on *pain au chocolat* and cheese.

Day Seven

My plan is to increase my barefoot time by two minutes a day but for the first two minutes today it seems impossible. As I start to run each step makes me feel like wincing and shouting 'ouch'. I can feel my body clenching, starting with a ball of tension at the top of my spine, so I consciously try to relax and concentrate on lifting rather than landing. Slowly it starts to feel better. I manage nine minutes, then think about the kind of pain women put their feet through all the time. This is a barefoot walk in the park compared to the agony I've experienced and seen others put themselves through in towering heels at the average wedding or night out.

A different kind of agony kicks in when I get back to the house. I've got a prickly heat rash on the tops of my feet, for which I'm blaming the trainers. My skin is bubbling and blistering as if I've scalded it and it's exquisitely itchy. Eventually I slather some *fromage frais* on my skin, then bathe them in cool water. The relief is immense. No more trainers for me. It could be a fanciful case of auto suggestion and a simple reaction to the nylon in a pair of cheap sports socks, but my body seems to be rejecting the trainers, like a skin it no longer needs.

Day Eight

I do eleven minutes barefoot running today. I still feel ridiculous doing it but it's less uncomfortable. The cycling is getting easier and more relaxing. Today I see a man with a pole with a bag on the top and a grabber attached. He's reaching the top branches of the roadside cherry trees to pluck the juiciest red cherries. It's a vignette I would have missed had I been zipping past in a car.

Day Nine

Thirteen minutes to and fro in front of the row of small houses in the suburbs of Quineville. I feel like a quirk in a French art house movie: the strange woman who, with no explanation, runs barefoot in front of the house of the hero at the same time every day as a family drama unfolds inside. Running barefoot on tarmac is still uncomfortable but feels easier, a little easier rather than a lot easier.

Day Ten

I'm waiting for the ET moment: the bit in the Spielberg movie where they are pedalling like blazes on their bikes and ET uses his alien magic to take them soaring into sky, the breakthrough moment when it feels like effortless flying. Today my sister in law comes with me to cycle down to Quineville. Midway down she gets a puncture and it's time to take my training to the next level. The puncture has happened serendipitously on a velvet smooth stretch of French tarmac. I have been looking at it ever since we arrived. It's just over a mile long, the white lines stencilled on it perfectly, hardly a piece of gravel on its black surface. It's like a model road, a perfect road. And today I step on to its warm smooth surface in bare feet. It feels as good as it looks and I run alongside Trish as she runs in trainers. Before long I've done more than a mile and a half, barefoot and without having to stop and change direction every minute or so. It's great. My calves are a little stiff when I finish, but nothing like they were ten days ago. I can use this mile of perfect road as a training stretch now. Bewildered French drivers may think I'm running from a house fire or an accident, barefoot and vulnerable. But no one has stopped or done anything other than sound a warning horn as they approach me to overtake.

In the days that follow I get to know this stretch of perfect French road as well as I know my own street. I see roadkill in various states of decomposition, feel the whoosh of lorries thundering towards Cherbourg and find wild cherries growing on the trees. They're soft and delicate, like apricots inside, nothing like the deep purple supermarket ones. Slowly I keep running. One mile up and one mile back to the bike with a little bit left over. I know where the piece of broken glass is and the exact spot where there's a drink can embedded in the tarmac (presumably the contents sucked down by a road worker, then the can tossed into the still warm tar). The song 'Turning Japanese' is on a loop in my head. It's 180 beats per minute, the number of steps per minute recommended for barefoot running. It's three steps a second, fast and constant, and I find it impossible to keep up. My workout time drops to around 50 minutes to allow for just under two and a half barefoot miles on this beautiful but busy stretch of tarmac. Sometimes cyclists pass me. One stares wide eyed at my bare feet padding along the road.

Day Fifteen

It's the midway point and the last day of the holiday. I treat myself to a beach run, getting to Quineville just in time as the tide starts to come in. The sand is cool and firm underfoot, with plenty of sharp shells to keep me careful. It's early enough for me to have the beach to myself. Fourteen days ago I struggled along this stretch and wrecked my calves after twenty minutes' barefoot running. Today I can run at my fastest pace for more than five minutes, slow to a stroll for a couple of minutes and go like the clappers again. In just two weeks I can see an improvement in how my heart is coping with aerobic exercise. It's taking me longer to get to my maximum heart rate and my recovery seems faster.

After thirty minutes the tide has sucked the last of my running surface away and it's back on the bike for a breakfast of coffee and croissants. I've burned an average of around 400 calories a day as I've learned to walk, then run barefoot. An average croissant contains around 200 calories so I'm not expecting any weight loss at the DCU weigh in.

Home today on an overnight ferry and a pair of barefoot shoes awaits me to let me take this new type of running to the footpaths and parks of Dublin. It will be nice not to have French men in BMWs zooming past with inches to spare as I run. Starting an exercise programme on holiday has been great. Instead of sitting over the third glass of wine and vowing to change things as soon as I get home I've changed them already. Taking the running back to the routine of house, work and children will be like taking a part of this holiday home. We are all filled with good intentions on the homeward journey. I hope I'm able to fulfill them in the next fifteen days.

Day Sixteen

Home and I'm struggling into my barefoot shoes (two words that are difficult to type without irony overload). They are as weird as they sound. Someone who was on holiday in London described seeing a man on the tube wearing a pair and moved warily away from him to travel in the next carriage.

I can see why. They *are* creepy. They look like diving shoes, a replica gorilla foot with padding on the sole where your foot is naturally padded at the sole and heel. Each toe has a separate rubber and fabric sleeve. It's a bit like trying to fit each toe into the leg of a pair of skinny jeans. I'm reminded of a friend who remarked in surprise several years ago how chubby my toes were (for a skinny girl).

Several red faced minutes later, the shoes are on and I'm off out my front door and running on the footpath. At first they're brilliant, like bringing the beach to the mean streets of the city. I still need to scan the path for gravel or glass but not so closely that I can't relax into the run. I can see why the advice is not to start in these but they are getting me to where I want to go. I run slowly to Stephen's Green, then run through. I even get in a bit of shopping at the end of the run. I'm glad that I have the shoes, weird and all as they are. A barefoot attempt on Dunne's Stores would probably be resisted by their door staff. I've bought a carton of eggs and put it into my backpack for the run home. It feels very Karate Kid to be running with a box of eggs on my back, ensuring I don't bounce too much. I get home with six intact eggs. Fifty yards from the house I slip off the shoes. My toes have started to feel sore, as if someone has tied a string around the base of each one. Instantly I'm back on holiday mode as I pad barefoot up my road to the house. It feels good. At the start of the run I thought I was definitely on the minimalist shoe side of the running fence. Now I see how attractive hardcore barefoot running is. Tomorrow I'm going to try it without the shoes in Stephen's Green.

Day Seventeen

I once walked into Stephen's Green with a drug addict who was carrying several deals of heroin. We made our way through the bushes to a hidden area of the park. He cooked up the drug on a filthy spoon, turned away for rudimentary privacy and injected it into a vein in his groin. I wrote about it as part of an account of a day with a drug addict in *The Irish Times*. Today I'm standing at the Harcourt Street entrance doing something that feels (somewhat obscenely) more illicit than those days as a crime reporter. I'm in my bare feet. I run a quick circuit of the park, avoiding the centre, but there are still plenty of people around. There is one other person not wearing shoes in the busy summer park – a footsore tourist sitting on a bench with his loafers unlaced and placed neatly side by side next to his feet. He's still got baby blue socks on and I am barefoot.

People stare. I think. I'm taking the same approach I did to public breastfeeding when my boys were babies. I'm concentrating so hard on what I'm doing that I don't have time to look around and gauge other people's reaction. It's pretty glorious running barefoot in Stephen's Green. In the sunny patches the smooth clean tarmac is warm like an under heated floor. In the shade it's cool. I imagine thousands of office workers coming to walk barefoot in this park as a break from the screen and the demands of their inboxes. I can't see it happening any time soon.

By the time I get home I've covered over four miles, according to MapMyRUN. It's strangely satisfying to replicate my run with mouse clicks on a map of Dublin. A red line traces where I've been and the mileage clicks up precisely in a clock at the top of the screen. A lap of the park is 0.66 of a mile. If I can increase my laps every second day I'll build up slowly and steadily.

Day Eighteen

A low point. My calves ache in a way that I know means I ran too far the previous day. My head hurts from trying unsuccessfully to navigate iTunes to download some 180 beats per minute tunes. For the first time in this project I don't want to go out the door for a run. My two younger boys clamber over me as if I'm a rock as I struggle to put on my barefoot shoes. Each time is as difficult as the first, not helped by the lovable small people. I'm grumpy and lumpen as I leave the house.

I'd love to say that all this disappears in a haze of endorphins five minutes into the run but it's not until I step barefoot on to the tarmac in Stephen's Green that I feel better. The ground is firm and cool and so implacably *there* under the skin of my soles that I feel grounded in a way I haven't been all day. It's very new age hippy stuff but there's something about walking in a city barefoot that's liberating and new.

Life has become an out of body experience for so much of our day. We live in the small rooms of our heads, hunched in spine seizing postures over keyboards for many hours at a stretch. It's great to get out of my head and into my feet. I do what few runners do while I run. I smile. Weirdo that I am. Smiling barefoot weirdo.

My brain does that thing it does when I'm exercising. A knotty problem about how to square a Sunday afternoon excursion with guilt about not spending enough time with the boys slowly unravels. When I run I can think straight. I sit on a bench beside the bronze statue donated to Ireland by the German government to put back on my tricky shoes. I smile gratefully at the park attendant who's picking up debris. He's the barefoot runner's best friend.

At one point in my run I imagine I have a super power. Running barefoot makes you feel like a superhero. Gravel is my kryptonite. Gravel and derision. The boost to my head makes my legs less heavy on the run home. I walk a good bit for the sake of the calves.

Today I sign up for a ten mile run in the Phoenix Park. It's happening five days after my thirty days are up so it seems like a goal. Perhaps an impossible one.

Day Nineteen

I am hanging up my bare feet. Today in the Phoenix Park was horrible. The older footpaths around the park are fine if you're wearing shoes, impossibly lumpy stretches of torture if you're not. The grassy paths which seem so cool just after a rain shower are strewn with branches, seeds, sharp shards of tree and other hazards mother nature has littered around. I am hobbling along trying to get over the pain and into the rhythm but it's not working.

I had resolved not to run today. I woke with stiff calves and feet as swollen as when I was in the latter stages of pregnancy. As I walked around the pain and swelling eased. So in the early evening I decided to bike to the Phoenix Park, the Shangri La of Dublin runners. The glare of sunlight on a wet road silhouetted the bike rider ahead of me as I waited to turn into the park. He was head to toe in lycra, lean as his wafer thin racer.

I start by walking and burst into occasional jogs up the main route, heading to the new bicycle lanes around the playing fields. Small children are playing football. A cricket game has begun. And everyone else who isn't driving through the park seems to be running. The lone runners look serious, like people who have bad news tucked in their snug lycra pockets. A more cheerful pack of runners passes, men and women, chatting loudly, a multi limbed running cluster of conviviality. I feel a pang of loneliness in my bare feet, struggle to put back on my minimalist shoes and continue.

After thirty minutes I give in, turn around and head back. A man in a yellow T shirt with 'Brisbane Marathon 2007' on it passed me on my run up and I noticed his elegant running style, a light forefoot strike in comfy trainers. He powers past me again. Mr Brisbane Marathon 2007. The lime green soles of his running shoes wink at me as he lifts them smartly. He is the quintessential running man, shaven headed, nut brown and anywhere between thirty and fifty. He makes it look fluid and effortless, years of running under his belt. A man like him is running in every park on the planet at every moment of the day and night. And I feel, as I watch him, I will never be him, or his female equivalent. For a while I try to use his bright yellow T shirt as a pacemaker but he's quickly swallowed by a tunnel of trees and I'm padding painfully back to my bike.

I need a rest. The leaves are starting to turn and fall to the ground. It's autumny for the first evening as I pedal disconsolately home. Two rest days, maybe three, then I'm back to the city centre. The Phoenix Park is too vast and full of serious runners for me.

Day Twenty Two
Back in the saddle and I'm running on the cool banks of the Grand Canal, which is swollen with rain from the night before. I've mapped a rough four mile route and I'm going to attempt it in my minimalist shoes. This morning I woke at 3am with that feeling that someone had just pulled the light switch cord in my brain. Ding. My heart was thumping for no apparent reason. Suddenly awake, I was full of negative thoughts and fears. Today I'm running away from my 3am self. It may have been the relaxed setting of the French holiday but every night I slept like a child and some nights I slept like a stone dropped into the bottom of a deep well. Every day on that holiday I did some taxing physical exercise. So today I'm going to run, whether or not my calf muscles like it. About a mile into the run the steel hands start to grip my calves in a way that would have made

me stop. But I have eight days to the end of this challenge and by day eight I want to be able to run these four miles without stopping. There are plenty of stretching places along the canal: railings, locks, bridges, where I can put my heel up, straighten my stiff legs and put my head to my knee. This is a beautiful running place. A moorhen and her chick walk in the grass and I stop to look at them. Her legs are lime greeny yellow, an astonishing colour I've never taken the time to notice before. The chick has long black legs and is a walking dust ball of fluff.

I love this run but with stops and stretches it takes me an hour, that's a fifteen minute mile, hardly faster than walking pace. At times I hobble and limp. When I take off my headphones I hear my feet slapping more loudly than I would have heard if I had not been listening to music. I may have to leave the music out of the running regime.

Day Twenty Three

I run again, even though my calves say no. I'm trying the traditional tough love approach of running through the pain until the muscles just accept that this is the way it is. It is against the barefoot creed of slow increments within your range. My sleep has changed radically since the holiday. The 3am and 4am wake up thing is happening again. I am lucky that I have no major worries in my life. The shape of my thoughts at that hour is like waking in a room that in daylight would be filled with friendly animals but at night all I can see are glinting eyes. It may be a natural rhythm of this training programme. There was such a sense of contentment for the first two weeks (helped by a wonderful holiday). Now I'm struggling to run while in pain and the season is shifting around us from summer to autumn. A yoga class tomorrow to stretch and breathe some of this tension out.

Day Twenty Five

It starts with the usual pain as I begin to run with an awkward, almost limping gait, then something seems to work better than before. I'm not saying I am an oiled machine but the slog shifts today into something approaching competence. It's a squally, showery evening but I leave the house in sunshine and a hoody. Five minutes into running I'm tying the hoody round my waist. It starts to rain and I like the feeling of drizzle on the skin of my arms. It rains more heavily and people put up umbrellas. It doesn't feel like a punishment but more like a pleasant part of being alive on an island on the North Atlantic. Anything that turns the rain into a gift is good. It's why I want to persist with this running, to try and find my inner runner. I have a canal and parks and historic streets in which to run and revel in being outdoors.

I remember suddenly the joy I found when I first tried running during my university days, the idea of being warm outside in the kind of weather we huddle to protect ourselves from and rush indoors to escape. I make my 4.6 miles in an hour, which makes it just under thirteen minutes a mile. I seem to have won the battle with my calves: they're flying a small white flag and saying OK. I'm tempted to increase my distance and keep going but I want to see how the muscles feel tomorrow. I stretched after I ran today (I watched a kick boxing tutor's calf and Achilles tendon stretch on YouTube). It's something I should do after every run. I want to be able to run again tomorrow.

Day Twenty Six

Five miles today. It feels like a breakthrough distance but I fear it may have pushed my calves into the pain zone again. It's nice to be running when the city is on the move. My run has fallen into the 5pm to 6pm rush hour slot. Waiting for the traffic lights to change turns the run into interval training, with my heart rate dropping quickly from its average of 150 beats to 120 per minute. I am tempted to skip a day's training, then try to run the ten mile course in the Phoenix Park before day thirty. I would be doubling my distance, which goes against the barefoot training technique of slow increments. I would like to get a feel for the route, to see whether any of it is smooth enough to run entirely barefoot.

I got word today that the DCU team can assess me on day thirty, four days from now. It will be a balance between training for the ten mile run and pushing so hard that I can't clamber up on to the treadmill to take the lung capacity test. Today's five hard miles have definitely given me more of an aerobic workout than slower, gentler runs. I am sleeping more deeply, exhausted every evening, and properly hungry for every meal I eat.

Day Twenty Eight

Back in the Phoenix Park and it's a friendlier place than when I last ran here. It's a Saturday morning and I'm going to run the ten mile course with my friend. We run gently and slowly around the route, following the map for next week's race. At times I stop and towards the end I take off my shoes as my toes are feeling swollen. The grass feels cool and silkily damp underfoot. There's a real sense of achievement and a set of aching muscles that tell us both we have pushed ourselves further than before.

Day Thirty

It's 8am and DCU campus is quiet. My artery test happens as before, with the stinging under tongue spray to change the lunar landscape of my blood vessels on the screen. Artery expert Sara Hughes has downloaded a speech by Daniel Lieberman from a US conference earlier that summer. He talks about an 'inactivity epidemic' in the US, where only 15 per cent of Americans are doing the required amount of exercise. We are all abnormal, he tells the audience. There is a mismatch between modern life and our palaeolithic bodies that were designed to run long distances every day.

On the scales I've gained one and a half kilos, bringing me to sixty two kilos. Muscle is heavier, they reassure me. I'm also mindful of my diet for the first two weeks, heavy in croissants and cream. On weight alone this could well count as a failure. But on the treadmill, running feels much more fluid. At eight kilometres an hour I don't feel the same sense of panic I did the previous time. The peak of the gradient is as tough as before and I wave a hand of surrender. I seem to have sweated more and when the post exercise blood sample is taken it gushes into the vial with a burst of froth.

Ironically, the fitter I was at the start the less dramatic any change is likely to be. I may not have aced the tests but I can feel a difference. I can run, steadily and for an extended amount of time. That's enough of a breakthrough for me.

Weeks later I get my test results. The quantity of endothelial particles thrown into my bloodstream by my panicked vascular system decreased by 20 per cent between day zero and day thirty, so my heart and vascular system are working more efficiently. I've reduced my resting heart rate from 60 to 56 beats per minute. At every stage in the running test my heart and lungs were working better, my heart beating at a lower rate. I may have gained weight but I have become fitter, demonstrably fitter. It's a result that the DCU scientists see across the board, from the teenage student and twenty something cohort to post cardiac arrest patients. Daily activity shows results. Do it every day and your body will get better at it.

Barefoot running may always remain a niche sector for hippy weirdo types like me. Asking regular runners to go without their beloved trainers (I think most runners grow to love their trainers) is almost like asking a cyclist to go without his or her bike. In Ireland we also have historical associations with being barefoot. Shoelessness is associated with shame, humiliation and disadvantage. Poverty and penance are what we think when we see someone barefoot anywhere other than on the beach. I love the fact that barefoot running is thoughtful running, a gentle approach that puts you entirely in touch with your surroundings.

The barefoot debate will rage on. Mainstream trainer companies like Nike and Adidas are now marketing minimalist shoes. It could be argued that the modern padded running shoe has enabled many more people to become runners than would otherwise have happened. But now there is a move back to basic plimsoll type shoes for running. Where there is a trend there is money to be made.

Comedian Eddie Izzard has started to run marathons barefoot, having previously completed forty three marathons in fifty one days. As a former wearer of high heels he's written funny accounts of his barefoot odyssey, including an attempt to run barefoot in Ethiopia where, at every turn, he was offered shoes. It will be interesting to see where this goes.

The Frank Duffy Ten Mile Race

The ground around the Papal Cross in the Phoenix Park is thronged with people. In the middle there's a blow up trainer the size of a car and the height of a double decker bus. They're selling trainers here. Everyone I can see is wearing trainers. At foot level it's a sea of white and gray and pink and neon running shoes. People jog and stretch and pile into one of three levels, fastest runners at the front. In the final wave, where I'm waiting, it's mostly women. We start slowly and most people run gently. No one is pounding the road. It's a beautiful sunny morning and it's a real pleasure being part of this great wave of running people.

Cruelly, on the first lap, we see the eight and nine mile markers for the faster runners who have already completed the first part of the run and are on their way to a second lap. A car pushes us to the right as the elite runners run past us. Jose Carlos Hernandez powers past. The Spanish runner, who is on his way to winning the race, is an anatomical drawing of lean muscle, tendon and bone, covered in a tight layer of skin. A Garda bike follows him. More than a dozen fast runners are in his wake. There is a type: wiry, legs slim from the knee down. Above the knees they have thick and powerful thighs. Their heels clip high behind them and they run on the fronts of their feet, forefoot striking. They are slicked head to toe in sweat. The sun keeps shining and the shade of trees is a balm. My heart rate has settled around 150 beats per minute. I can still talk, chatting to my friend as we run gently. The pace is set.

At the seven mile mark I can feel my toes throb painfully. Like cartoon feet, each one feels like a throbbing beacon of pain. It's time to go bare. Just short of three miles to go I sit on the grass and pull off my shoes. A green tarmac cycle path is smooth and gorgeous. The grass is cool and I can feel the soft mud underneath. The sensation is marvellous and I get an instant lift. I run the last two and a half miles in bare feet, slowing a little when the ground gets rough, worried that it will get so rough I will be forced to stop and put my shoes back on. But it's good. I can feel the asphalt beating back the heat of the sunny morning. At one bend a female steward commends my bare feet. 'That's the way to do this,' she says. Others are just bewildered by what I'm doing. By now the heaviness in my legs is gone and I know I'm going to run every mile. This could all be stopped by just a few yards of gravel on the road but so far it's been good. I can't stop smiling.

At the finish line the commentator has settled into welcoming the stragglers home. At the sight of me his voice rises slightly. 'And here comes someone running in her bare feet,' he says. 'It's… (a slight pause as he checks my number)…Catherine Cleary. Well, Catherine Cleary. You're some woman. Now go over there and buy yourself a pair of trainers.'

Four thousand five hundred and thirty three runners have come in before me but I've done the run in one hour and fifty three minutes, roughly eleven minutes per mile. It's not a time to set anyone's heart racing but it's my fastest pace since I started this. And with the last three miles barefoot it's been a beautiful run.

Running felt impossible when I started this just over thirty days ago. Now it is possible. The tyranny of running is that I need to keep doing it if I'm to keep those muscles working. Dropping it for any length of time means a return to that stage where running feels impossible again. I have no desire to run a marathon but I want to be able to walk out my front door, break into a gentle run and come back fifty or sixty minutes later refreshed and calm.

Five months later I'm still running. On a good day I can run an eight minute mile. I take a radio, tune it to RTÉ Lyric FM and escape into a serene and mainly bad news free zone. I have pulled on my barefoot shoes to pad the streets of Copenhagen, New York, the Faroe Islands and Swinford in County Mayo. I may not be a Mr Brisbane Marathon 2007 but I am a runner. And this summer I discovered that you don't need the landing beaches of Normandy to start barefoot running. On the beach in Enniscrone in County Sligo you can run a 5km round trip barefoot, then wade through an ice cold sea current, like a racing horse in a pool, cooling and relaxing tired muscles.

Postscript

After months of barefoot running I pushed myself too hard one day and ended up with Achilles tendon stiffness. Then I ran awkwardly to save that leg and pulled a calf muscle in the other leg. Barefoot running doesn't prevent injuries and every time you want to run further or faster you have to increase in tiny amounts. I found a sports physio, David Ukich, who is a barefoot runner. Growing up in Western Australia he spent his childhood running around barefoot. He's fascinated not only by the debate in the running shoe industry but by the huge market for orthotics, stiff plastic supports prescribed for people (and now children) suffering from foot and back problems. The muscles, tendons and strength I needed to run barefoot could take twelve months to build up, he advised me. So the 'slowly gently' running approach has to be applied at every step, even when I felt I had mastered it. That means increasing speed or distance by no more than 10 per cent a week.

I took my time and distance back to scratch again, listening to my muscles and letting them dictate how far and fast I ran. Slowly I built myself up to being able to run for between forty five minutes and an hour. As yet I have no joint pain and my niggly left knee has been fine. I still get people doing double takes at my weird footwear but at every big race I've done since August I've spotted a fellow barefoot traveller or two.

The single best gear investment has been a large foam roller, which I use to roll out my aching calf muscles before and after a run. I should have bought one on day one. It's been more valuable to me than any other piece of kit. If you want to become a runner, any type of runner, get a foam roller and use it.

5

Horse, Horse, Tiger, Tiger

I must have been a pain for my busy parents. A clingy shy teen, prone to homesickness, I dug in my heels in at the prospect of a French summer exchange. I always refused to go and live in someone else's house and get that full immersion experience of another language. No Irish college or sitting at the dinner table of a French family eating strange food, just summers hanging around the local tennis courts or the house and begging for lifts everywhere.

My one brief experience of being thrown in at the deep end with a foreign language was a postgraduate summer in Paris in 1994. I got a grant to spend three months at the Centre de Formation et de Perfectionnement des Journalistes (CFPJ) There were no formal courses going on but I was given the run of the college darkrooms and I had a thesis to finish. I spent all my spare francs in the photography department of the Les Halles branch of the department store Fnac buying chemicals and photographic paper.

Digital photography was on the horizon but newspapers still had darkrooms where photographers developed and printed their pictures for that day's paper. I spent long happy hours printing the photographs for my series of magazine essays around the planned redevelopment of Temple Bar as an artists' and residential quarter. In the end Temple Bar would be turned into a drinking quarter and newspaper darkroom equipment all over the world would be thrown into skips.

I went to Paris with rusty schoolgirl French and found that I was almost at a standing start when it came to making myself understood in real life. My first forty eight hours in the city left me at sea as I trekked around with a heavy rucksack, heat beating off the pavements, looking for a hotel I could afford. I finally rang the only contact I had in the city, the mother of a cousin's pen pal and French exchange friend. Françoise Noir was then working as a headmistress in a suburban school. She met me off the metro, took me out for a crêpe and gave me a room in her apartment rent free.

In an attempt at thanks for her generosity I helped paint her apartment one weekend. She had a dog called Gauloises, after her favourite brand of cigarette, and his hair stuck in clumps on the pink gloss paint as we painted in the heat of that Paris summer. Françoise spoke English but preferred to speak French. As a teacher she was the perfect host for a linguistically challenged guest.

My mornings were spent in the college dark rooms and afternoons were for people watching, taking pictures, writing postcards and letters home and exploring Paris. In a way that few exchange students are now I was entirely removed from home. There was no Internet access to read Irish newspapers, Skype calls or Facebook status updates. I couldn't watch English language programming on a laptop. There were occasional brief, expensive phone calls and lots of letters.

Within a few weeks I could understand much of what people were saying to me. It took a while longer to drum up the courage to speak. A glass of wine or a beer was always an aid to fluency. I remember wondering whether I would ever be fluent enough in another language to form thoughts in that language, so that it was a French word I would think of first before its English equivalent.

That summer in Paris seems magical, looking back. Darkrooms with their vinegary tang of developers and fixers are now the domain of the art student and enthusiastic amateur. Much like the slow food movement, a slow picture movement might reawaken skills that have been jettisoned. I fondly remember the patient swimming into being of an image, hours or even days after it was taken, rather than seeing it immediately on a screen. There was a sense of mystery and potential about what was in a camera's undeveloped film, those small black canisters that we put into envelopes and posted, not so long ago, to receive a thick wedge of prints a short time later. Those thesis shots were the last pictures on which I would lavish any time. When I returned I started a work experience stint in *The Irish Times*, then began freelancing. Any language skills I had were shelved in the busy years that followed and my French dwindled back to holiday scraps, almost as if it had never existed.

Now I had decided to try to learn Mandarin, the official language of China. I could have signed up for a refresher French course or taken on Spanish, Italian or German. But I wanted to push the limits of my learning by taking on an entirely alien language, one in which there would be no familiar sounds or guessable words to build on. Mandarin words would be as new to me as language is to a newborn and they would stretch my brain, kicking away its Google crutch, and making it struggle to learn something entirely new in a way that felt daunting and, at times, utterly impossible.

As I prepared to take on the learning challenge I realised the problem was that I had outsourced my memory to machines. This dawned on me when I dropped my bog standard mobile phone and smashed the screen. The phone still worked but only as a phone. People could ring me and I could make calls. But with a broken screen I could only phone two people, my husband and my mother, because I couldn't remember a single other number. The others were gone. Even the numbers of my closest friends and family were lost behind the black murk of the leaky LCD screen. I had keyed them into my phone, trusted the technology to take care of them and let them go.

A simple theory of neuroscience is that memory is like a muscle. If we stop using it, relying on it to remember things, it becomes flabby and inefficient. Technology has taken the burden of memory off our shoulders. Remembering things has suddenly become something we no longer need to do, like handwashing clothes or peeling potatoes.

The labour saving device of the Internet keeps everything anyone might need to remember at any given time at our fingertips, assuming we have Internet access. But I wonder how this is affecting me and if it would be good to make myself memorise things again as I did when I was a child? To take some things back from the technological ether and make them 'possessions of the soul'?

The phrase comes from Herman Ebbinghaus, a German psychologist who died in 1909. He is the father of the concept of a learning curve, a forgetting curve and the idea of 'distributed learning', or doing a little every day.

Ebbinghaus was fascinated by human memory. Using himself as the subject of his experiment he devised a system of nonsense syllables to test his own ability to remember. During an experiment he would set a metronome ticking on his desk and pull out random nonsense syllables from a box. He read out syllables with the same tone and inflection, then attempted to remember them and write them down in the same sequence, keeping detailed logs of how long it would take to remember them. He found a steep decline in memory in the first twenty minutes but if he tried to reremember the sequence twenty four hours after first learning it, memorising took him a third less time. Ebbinghaus found that refreshing memory for a short period of time each day was an efficient way of learning. In 1885 he published his research in a book called *Memory, A Contribution to Experimental Psychology*. His century old research and the more recent discoveries of neuroscience support the idea of a daily routine.

Most of Ebbinghaus's book is written in the dry language of a nineteenth century scientist, with mathematical formulae to try to quantify his results. But there are occasional lapses into something more poetic. 'If the relearning is performed a second, a third or a greater number of times,' he wrote, 'the series are more deeply engraved and fade out less easily and finally as one would anticipate, they become possessions of the soul.'

The idea that a memory, or a nugget of information, can become part of a person by being threaded into their 'soul' may seem fanciful. In the copy of Ebbinghaus's book I read someone had firmly written the word 'mind' over the deeply unscientific term 'soul'. But the science of the brain tells us that laying down memories more permanently than life's many fleeting impressions is a physical process. Making memories changes the structure of the brain. It's a deeper way of processing information, turning our memories into a physical part of who we are.

The words of Mandarin would be as alien to me as Ebbinghaus's nonsense syllables. Whether I could weave them into the fabric of my brain was going to be the challenge.

Professor Shane O'Meara has taken more DART trips than he can remember. In fact nearly all his DART trips have melted into a blobby mass of generic DART journeys. Most mornings on his way to his office in Trinity College, his senses take in the choppy waves or the glassy calm of the Irish Sea, the sounds of the train, other people's music, the rustle of newspapers, the occasional cough. Yet very little of this sensory information lodges in his memory. Few permanent memories attached to that time, that morning, that train taking him and hundreds of others to school, college or work. Like billions of humans on the planet the professor has a routine, a groove or a furrow that he follows on a working day. Pedestrians in New York, commuters on the Tokyo underground, teeming masses of individuals move together, catching regular morning trains, seeing the same people pushing buggies on pavements, walking or cycling or driving the same familiar route. Those morning and evening routes blend into a gist memory. We know we came to work on the train this morning but we'd be hard pressed to remember any particular detail of the journey.

Professor O'Meara is the head of Trinity College's neuroscience department and one of the country's leading experts on how our brains learn new things, store memories and function as we age. I wanted to ask him about the science of learning: whether at forty one years old, I could really acquire a new skill or language as easily as a child might and if I were going to try it how best to go about it.

The first thing I asked was whether the idea of trying something every day was a good one.

'One of the things that a hundred years of experimental psychology has taught us is that doing a little often is better than doing a lot infrequently,' he says. 'The classic example is student's idea of pulling an all nighter as being the best way to study for an exam. It's not. The brain learns incrementally and doing something every day is really the best way to go about it rather than doing a lot one day. If you are trying to learn a piece of prose and you do an hour a day for seven days you'll learn substantially more than if you spend seven hours in one day.'

The research indicates that it is what we do in between the times we are learning that is important for our ability to retain the information. 'It's increasingly clear in the last five years in particular that doing something every day involves an important event that happens every day, which is that you go to bed and you go to sleep,' Professor O'Meara said. 'And we now know, with almost a racing certainty, that regular periods of nightly sleep are absolutely required for memories that are accumulated during the day to become consolidated.'

Like any daily activity that requires effort, building memories is energy intensive. 'It requires that the connections between brain cells become remodelled. This takes a lot of effort. It burns up a lot of energy. You need to make new proteins in the brain, restructuring the brain, and it looks like evolution has selected sleep as the time for us to do that,' Professor O'Meara explained. 'Children do most of their growing when they're asleep. The elaboration of the networks of the brain happens very very intensively in young children and it continues to happen in later life.

'The overall purpose of sleep is kind of a mystery. It turns out that every species does it. So behaviour that's that widespread must play a very important role. But it isn't obvious what it is. We know what digestion is for. It's perfectly obvious why we eat. But it's not perfectly obvious why we sleep. But we do know that sleep deprivation leads to all sorts of appalling problems. Extended sleep deprivation can result in feelings of psychosis. Sleep deprivation increases stress hormones in the bloodstream. It can lead to people having terrible problems regulating blood sugar.'

The other factor that neuroscience and anecdotal evidence tell us is that the more you know the easier it is to learn. So starting something completely new is 'very difficult at the start'. But as the brain begins to lay down knowledge it paves the way for easier learning.

I'm also interested in asking Professor O'Meara about the effect on our brains of the Internet and the world of information at our fingertips. The night before I went to see him I sat down to try and complete a newspaper crossword. It felt like being asked to walk down a supermarket aisle with both hands tied behind my back, picking up what I needed only with my teeth. My brain ached trying to reach for the word that I felt matched the clue. My fingers itched to tap it into the nearest keyboard or hand held device. Confined to paper and pencil, my Google brain was limping without its crutch. In a very few years computers and smartphones have become the portals to all knowledge. Why carry information in your head when it's in your pocket? Technology has made research easier but in other ways it has hobbled me.

And then there is the distraction epidemic. 'A lot of the things that are pressing for your attention are things that you can just ignore,' Professor O'Meara explained. 'People feel that writing an email is getting work done but of course it's not.' It's a point of view that stems from working in academia, where producing papers, researching or preparing lectures are the units of productive work, rather than scheduling meetings or agreeing things in online communication with others. 'I think people need to be very disciplined with emails. I have to admit I'm not very disciplined. I have a smartphone and emails chase me all over the place. You become known as someone who responds very quickly so you get a lot thrown at you.'

He puts his smartphone in another room if he is working on academic research. Otherwise he finds himself checking the phone at the end of every page he's reading.

Even as I sit here and type I can feel the tug to log on and check my emails. The lure is strong to unspool my focus and let my kite brain fly over the world of the Internet, lighting on this website or this tweet or that blog. But the more time I spent flitting around the Internet the more I found the front of my head ached. I would float between Twitter and email and any number of favourite websites. I would finish the 'one quick look', then begin the process again, just to see what had changed since I last looked. Very quickly I would find the precious hours when my children were at school or my child minder was in charge had gone, with nothing to show for them other than a mild feeling of anxiety and an ache in the front of my head.

Often I have reached down and physically switched off my broadband connection in order to make it more difficult to click away from the page I am writing. In order to find out if someone wants to sell me Viagra or a designer dress I can't afford (the bulk of my emails) I will have to reach down and switch it on again, then reboot the computer. I can usually talk myself out of doing that more easily than I can resist the urge to move the mouse and click.

Midway through this project I bought a new computer. Its word processing package allowed me to click the page so that everything behind the words I was writing faded to black. Although I know the Internet icon is there I can't see it all the time. It's as close as you can get to pretending to write on a typewriter with a blank piece of paper on the roller.

Major companies have instituted quiet time (back to that nannyish nursery term) for employees, a stretch of time in the morning when Internet access is limited. Increasingly (especially for a journalist) the Internet is a tool of work so it is left to us to put those boundaries around our time, to install some quiet time in our routines when we can get things done. Now I find I can write for long stretches only if writing is the first thing I do when I switch on the machine. If I go straight online my focus is lost, I have loosened the strings on the kite and I find the tugging power of distraction irresistible.

Is it all making us more stupid as a race? I asked Professor O'Meara. He has an optimistic take on it. 'If anything we're getting smarter. If you took IQ tests administered in the 1920s and gave them to students now they are above where they were in the 1920s. The test makers have to regrade the IQ tests every generation or so.'

'My nephew Facebooked me this morning to find out how he could hook up a piece of computer to something else. Now I knew what a computer was when I was twelve but I didn't own one. He's got four or five of them lying around. He's growing up in an environment where children are better fed, better educated and better stimulated than they were before. Look at the quality of textbooks now compared to older ones, the learning aids available. We might be lazy but the route to laziness is the creative thinking about how to create shortcuts.'

Will all that privilege and advantage be lost in the all consuming distraction of the Internet? Is it just my middle aged brain that is being fried by the Internet and will someone raised with a chubby baby finger on a tablet screen be better able to juggle the demands on their attention? Can we focus on anything any more?

'A study has just appeared on the use of ebooks as tools for learning and it turns out that ebooks are sub optimal. It turns out that we have different representations in our minds for a book,' O'Meara explained. He picked up a book from his desk. 'This is a large five hundred page book. And there's the content. Obviously in an ebook I can flip through the pages. But there's also a depth to a book and people have multiple methods of representing information. When people think about a book they think about the knowledge organised physically in topographic terms. I know the chapter I've been reading is probably about halfway through and if I think about what I've been learning from this book I'll mentally journey to that halfway point. I don't have to go and look up the table of contents to find it. I know that it's about there because we interact with the text in a physical way.'

Anyone writing a research paper can spread eight or ten books on a table, an impossibility with an ebook even on a large computer screen. 'I think we're going to find that it's going to become another tool, for the trashy novels I'll take off on summer holidays. But for books you're going to repeatedly work with and refer to, I can imagine people won't want to use ebooks.'

'Wait till you find yourself in place where you don't have access to the Internet. Books and paper, as it turns out, are mighty pieces of technology.'

Our brains like learning, it seems, just like our bodies like exercise. Once over the difficult initial and early stages of learning something new, the brain becomes better at taking on more information. In other words the more you learn the better you become at learning. And I believe that in the absence of learning our busy active minds will find other things to do, like worry incessantly or turn up the volume and complexity of the negative voice in our heads that chips away at contentment, one caustic drip at a time.

'I'm a movie buff and I love talking about movies,' O'Meara said, explaining that brains that have already worked hard at something can continue to do it more easily. 'I can retain material about a film very easily. I have a friend who's into jazz into a very serious way. He plays the trumpet and I'm amazed at his knowledge and expect that he recalls things very easily because he's got a very elaborate schema, a kind of pre existing set of hooks that knowledge can be hung on to. In other words the more that you know the easier it is to learn more about a field. As you become more expert there's an acceleration in your ability to learn about the area you're interested in.'

And is there a saturation point? 'Really the limit where expert knowledge is concerned comes down to issues of motivation and judgement. If you're going to learn a new language for an hour a day that's only thirty hours [in thirty days]. A child exposed to a language community takes, they listen, they practise sounds for two or three years before they utter properly spoken words. So that's a lot of hours. Then they acquire the language and they learn a hundred words a day. And that's a lot. But the brain at that point is pre prepared to acquire language. This is the major different between children and adults. There are critical periods for particular types of learning and if you're not exposed to the necessary environment at that time you won't get that knowledge. The simple example is language itself. Children need to be exposed to the language community pretty much from birth, continuously, for a period of several years in order to be able to learn to speak. There are tragic examples of children raised in near feral circumstances or who are deaf for the first four or five years of life and they find it astonishingly difficult to acquire a new language.'

So even though I might learn a new language I would be unlikely ever to speak it with a native accent, as the window for the part of my brain to acquire the music of a language shuts in early childhood.

The other good thing about my idea of trying something new intensively for thirty days is that it will puncture the gist memory haze we can fall into. Those DART journeys that blur into one, or plane journeys by frequent travellers, make memories difficult to locate. The older we get the harder it seems to get to remember the specific date we did something. Did I go to that restaurant for my thirty sixth or thirty seventh birthday?

You can plant landmarks in your life by moving out of your comfort zone and trying something entirely new, making your brain grapple with unfamiliar territory again. 'Going and doing things that are out of the norm, these are very good things for you, in motivational and cognitive terms. New experiences are good things to chase in that sort of sense.'

I left Professor O'Meara's office with a list of six dos for the challenges to come:

1.   Get a good night's sleep.
2.   Get regular aerobic exercise.
3.   Practise every day.
4.   Test yourself every two or three days.
5.   Rehearse what you've done the day before you start the new day's learning.

and

6.   Be very happy to make mistakes.

The final point is interesting. We are conditioned not to embrace mistakes but to cover them up, blame others or rationalise them away. 'Learning is error driven,' Professor O'Meara said, 'something that people don't appreciate very much. We don't learn very much from our successes. We learn an awful lot from our failures. Be willing to tolerate your failures because for learning something they're very important. The older and more established we get in our chosen field the harder it is to start something new so we tend to avoid the frustrations of mastering a new skill.'

The professor cited the example of the successful businessman who throws his tennis racquet or golf club in the air in frustration and walks away thinking, 'I'm an expert at what I do and everybody respects me. Here I am trying to hit a ball and it lands in the wrong place. I should be able to do this. Godammit, I'm brilliant at everything else.'

But actually it's those frustrations and mistakes that keep our brains healthy. And there will be a lot of them in the next thirty days as I take on Mandarin.

Day One

The last time I walked down Merrion Square carrying an orange folder I was on my way to an antenatal visit in the National Maternity Hospital. This time I'm heading to a language school and the orange notebook is a cheap foolscap notepad I bought in the dash to make it on time. I'm on my way to my first Chinese lesson. The language school is behind the heavy yellow door of one of the grand houses on this elegant city square.

Grace Mullins is sitting on a bench in the tiled hallway. She's a very pleasant young Chinese woman dressed casually in a red jumper and black trousers. We smile and shake hands and start up the impressive white painted staircase. From the top floor a smaller staircase takes us up to the attic rooms. There's a cast iron fireplace in the narrow room, which was probably once a bedroom for the housemaids who kept this large household running, and a great view out the sash window of the treetops of the park in Merrion Square.

We sit on either side of the narrow row of tables and I explain my idea. I think I am her first student with no plans to go to China. Past students have all been learning Mandarin before they head to China to negotiate business or diplomatic life.

I have spoken to others who have tried to learn Mandarin about how difficult they found it. In my mind the language challenge has turned into a stone wall: smooth, enormous and, with no toe or hand holds, impossibly different and more difficult than anything I can imagine.

Mandarin is now the official Chinese language, with Cantonese relegated to second place. In writing, both languages look very similar, Grace explains. The spoken languages are very different. Grace starts slowly, explaining the difference between the pinyin, or phonetic way of writing Mandarin, and the characters, the elaborate word pictures which Chinese children learn when they first learn to read and write. I wonder if 'pinyin' is the origin of the term 'Pidgin' English, the simplified code that developed as a means of communication between speakers of English and languages like Chinese. We all know those Chinese symbols in black, elegant swirls of ink, which can form words or parts of words. On every street they are displayed, usually in a red lit sign over the local Chinese takeaway. The pinyin words are further subject to five tones which change the meaning of identical words to something entirely different.

'You never need to close your mouth at the end of the word,' Grace explains, as no words end with the hard staccato consonant sounds we know. Western languages bite words out of the air. This language is more about flow, words coming through an open mouth. You can speak Chinese and smile at the same time. I feel it could suit our soft 't' and Irish way of slurring words rather than enunciating them with a rhythmic precision. Later I realise that Chinese, or spoken Mandarin, may not have hard endings to its words but has its own staccato rhythm that is not part of the way we speak English.

The tones, too, are musical. The third tone (which appears like a dip above the letter) tells you to bring your voice down, then up again. It's a little like a Cork accent. A straight line above a letter lengthens the vowel sound. A slanted line like a *fada* indicates an upward lilt. A line slanting downwards, left to right, is like a chopping sound, cutting the word dead. What makes it fiendishly complex is the fact that each enunciation or tone changes the meaning of identical words. So the word *ma* can change from 'mother' to 'horse' depending on the tone.

At one point Grace draws the Chinese character for the word 'country' or 'kingdom'. It's to explain the way China is written as two characters, meaning 'middle kingdom'. The character for 'kingdom' starts with a doorway and inside she draws two short lines, then a longer line goes down from the top and is finished with a short base line. On the base line she places a dot. She finishes the doorway by turning it into a rectangle. The enclosure or rectangle represents land, she explains, the character inside is a king and the dot is the jade or jewel in his crown. It's simple and beautiful.

I finish by reading some short sentences and we resolve to greet each other in Chinese the following morning. 'Hello' (or *Ni hao* which means literally 'You good?') becomes 'How are you?' with the addition of *ma* at the end (literal translation 'you good eh?'). *Ma* in this case is neither a horse nor a mother but the word that turns a statement into a question. Not all questions need to have *ma* at the end. I practise the question and answer on my bike, smiling the words into the wind of the blustery autumn day as I go and trying not to sound like a B movie Chinaman.

I'm looking more closely at the Chinese characters on takeaway restaurant signs around the city. Every now and again I can see the symbols for the middle kingdom on the red and yellow neon signs.

Day Two

This is difficult but enjoyable. Over the coming days I am going to take twenty hours of lessons, try to work on my own on days I don't have lessons and do my homework and revision each night. My memory grapples with these strange new words and symbols. When I learn the numbers it is the characters that are easier to remember. The words for 'one, two, three' keep slipping from my head. The symbols are much easier – a single dash for one, two dashes for two with a shorter one on top and three dashes for three, two of equal length and one shorter one in the middle. At home at the kitchen table I write and draw them in a list. Slowly they sink in. I read them to my eldest son. He is able to repeat them back to me after one reading. An elastic mind. Mine is feeling more like old dozed rubber. But I keep at it. I need forty minutes of homework to get the numbers into my head as well as the extra words of vocabulary.

There is a twin track of effort, firstly to pronounce the word, with its very different consonant and vowel sounds, then to grasp the meaning of the word.

Names are central to Chinese culture. My name in Chinese would be *Kai se lin*. It's quite a popular name in China, Grace tells me, thanks to the Hollywood star Kathryn Hepburn. Most Chinese people in the west have two names, their Chinese name and their western name. Grace was originally called Xiao e (pronounced 'Schaw Uh') and like most Chinese first names hers is full of meaning, translated as 'goddess of the morning', because she was born early in the morning. Her second name was *Deng*, so her name would be given in Chinese as *Deng Xiao e*. Families in China put enormous thought into naming their children, not least because of the one child policy. It would be disrespectful to the child to give them the name of their father or mother. Instead their name says something unique about them, the circumstances of their birth, their parents' hope for them or dreams for their future.

The stereotype of the Chinese tiger mother is close to the truth of what many Chinese parents expect of their children. 'Chinese parents are not willing to give up on their children,' Grace explains. Small children spend hours of their lives learning to draw the intricate Chinese characters, one stroke at a time, in small copybooks with squared lines ruled on them.

If they move to the west Chinese people often shed their beautiful meaning filled names, like a skin. Sometimes there will be a westernised version available to them but in Xiao e's case she chose an entirely new name. So Deng Xiao e became Grace Mullins.

Numbers are very important, she explains. You need to know them and wield them in every transaction. Unless you bargain in China you will pay ten times more than the price. In later lessons it will be clear how central numbers are in Chinese culture, more so than in the west.

Day Three

This is beginning to feel like trying to learn to swim by putting my foot in a basin of water. I get the brief sensation of wetness and floating but there is no immersion. When I leave the upper room in Merrion Square I don't walk into a babble of Chinese, hearing the tones and the rhythm of the speech all around me, that immersion in a language that comes from daily transactions with paper sellers or shop assistants. A subtitled television programme I tried to watch one evening, about a travelling Chinese judge arbitrating disputes in remote rural communities, was dispiriting. The only word I recognised was the word *ma* at the end of a sentence to indicate that it was a question. Grace reassures me that if the people were speaking a dialect she too would need to read the subtitles to understand what they were saying.

Today there is more about numbers and the tradition and culture built around them. Six, eight and nine are lucky numbers in China because they sound like the words for smoothness, prosperity and eternity. The number four is despised, even more unlucky that our western thirteen because it sounds like the word for death. Number superstition is built into everyday Chinese life. Mobile phone numbers and car registrations containing the lucky numbers come at a premium.

Day Four

We spend a long time going through the pronunciation of pinyin words. As a tonal language, spoken Chinese can sound flat, the expression in the voice saved for the tones. I'm finding my schoolday Irish and French bubbling up from under the rusted over surface of my language ability. The words for 'she is' or 'he is', *ta shi*, sound very like the Irish *tá sí* (in the case of Irish the 'eee' sound is longer at the end of *sí*. The Chinese *shi* is pronounced like 'shit' without the 't'). But in Chinese the *ta* is the person (he or she) and the *shi* is the verb 'to be'. Ireland is *ai er lan*. Now I can say, 'I am an Irish person': *Wo shi ai aer lan ren* (literally, 'I am Ireland person.') The 'r' sound on the word *ren* for person is the one that gets lost in translation in both directions. In spoken Mandarin it comes out like a rolling *sche* sound. For this you have to curl up the front of your tongue and roll the sound gently in the back of your mouth.

Day Seven

I make faces today. I screw my eyes up tightly and look at the ceiling. I puff and grunt and grimace. It's far from pretty. I'm trying to remember the words and phrases I last looked at three days ago. I wonder at the faces we make as we struggle to winkle something out of our memories. Grace widens her eyes when she speaks to me as if willing the words out through them. I, in turn, squint and screw up my eyes as I listen, trying to recognise the individual words I know in her slow, clear sentences.

As I leave the class today I realise that daily practice is the only way to make this language bed in. When I walk out into the fresh air of Merrion Square my head is full of Chinese words, flitting like butterflies. I need to net them and pin them down later by repeating them, writing them, putting them in sentences. Otherwise they flutter away, beautiful but impossible to remember.

Work and family life have pushed out the Chinese. At the weekend in a choice between an hour with *Downton Abbey* or an hour with Chinese homework I took the easy option. The result is that it's been three days since I opened my foolscap notebook and looked at these Chinese words. These days have rusted the gears in my brain. It feels physically taxing again to get things to stick.

Today I learnt the names of the months and days of the week which, apart from Sunday, are known only by their numbers, the order in which they come. Grace sees lots of English speaking students counting with their fingers to try to figure out which day of the week or which month they are talking about. So there is no word for October in Chinese. It is Ten Month. Tuesday is Weekday Two. It's beautifully simple but for an English speaker wedded to the idea of months and days with names it's a feat of memory to relate one language to the other without using fingers to count themselves through the transition.

On my run this evening I teach myself the days of the week, pacing out the three syllable words. Weekday One (Monday), Weekday Two (Tuesday)…in time to my running steps. It's still hard to name them out of sequence, or hear Weekday Five and know instantly that it's Friday. One new thing I learned today makes me think about our idea of time and how it passes. Instead of 'last year' the Chinese say the 'gone year', an idea that focuses what I'm trying to do. At its end the year is gone. Month One (a much more hopeful description than the western January) comes around and another year starts. In a few months' time 2011 will be the gone year, taking experiences with it, never to return.

Day Eight

I'm learning more country names in Mandarin, which is a little like seeing the world from another angle. America is *Mei Guo*, 'the beautiful kingdom', which Grace feels is a name to which Ireland could lay legitimate claim. Other place names are more prosaic. France is *Fa Guo*. Europe is *Ou Zhou* (which is pronounced a little like 'Oh Joe').

Greetings can be elaborate in Chinese and just as with French there is a more respectful way of saying 'you' with *ni* changing to *nin* if you are talking to an older person. There are at least two ways of asking someone's name. The informal question *ni xing shenme* translates as 'your family name what?' A more formal version of the question would be *nin guixing* or 'may I know your name?' The more elaborate way of saying 'hello' literally translates as 'to meet you very glad', a phrase that sounds anglicised to Grace's ears, an archaic sort of greeting like people saying 'pleased to meet you', little heard outside language classes and story books.

Today I also learn about a word that has no equivalent in English. It's the measure word, a word that has no meaning but must be put between the number and a noun. The most common measure word is *ge*. So one person is said as *yi ge ren* (one measure word person). The measure word changes according to the noun, which makes it sound even more complicated. For instance, if I want to talk about three books the measure word for book is *ben*.

Day Nine

My husband is my love person. At least that's the literal translation for spouse. Every day there is something in my Mandarin class that makes me smile. One friend talks about learning some basic Chinese from flatmates and remembering that 'I love you' or *wo ai ni* sounds like 'wall eye knee'.

The interesting thing about this process is how much easier I'm finding it to translate written words than spoken. I can look at a written pinyin word, some of the dozens that I'm beginning to write down to remember, and know its meaning immediately. When Grace speaks to me using that word I find it much more difficult to translate. If I miss the first words in a sentence as she talks to me I'm lost: I can't catch the tail of what she is saying to me and pick up the thread of the sentence. I find myself repeating her words back to myself slowly to try and piece it together. Her pronunciation is slow and careful and I'm still finding it hard to follow.

Later that day I'm in a changing room in a Gap shop and two Chinese women come into the room next door. They are chatting constantly and I listen, trying to catch the tail of some sentence, a word I might recognise. But I can't get a hold of anything. It may well be that they are Cantonese speakers or speaking in a dialect but their conversation is impenetrable.

I need to listen to more spoken Chinese. I've downloaded a 'newbie' class from Chinesepod, a virtual language school run out of China. The lessons are in the form of a conversation between the owner, Ken, and his female Chinese colleague. Each one has a preamble of Chinese music, which I find annoying, and the 'newbie' module is very basic. I've probably already covered everything in the first few podcasts but it's interesting to hear spoken Chinese. The approach is much more casual and the lessons are aimed at people driving, or running or doing something that means they can't sit down and write. It feels like a good partner to my intensive hour with pen and paper and words on the whiteboard. It's also interesting to hear the rhythm of spoken Chinese.

Day Ten

We had class earlier this morning and it was useful, as my brain seemed more able for new information. Studying at night it feels sluggish and tired. I'm constantly surprised by how tiring this learning is. I am physically exhausted by the end of each day. After every class I am ravenously hungry and have built a coffee and bun break into the post class routine.

Tonight at the dinner table my eight year old says hello in Chinese. I give the family a quick lesson in how to ask 'how are you?' and respond with, 'I'm very well.' My sons have a natural ability to remember things. Rote learning is a large part of my eldest child's homework. He repeats his spellings out loud and his maths tables rhythmically and quickly, to impress them on his memory.

I think part of my problem with the spoken language is self consciousness and the fear of sounding ridiculous. As a child you are better able to try out sounds and words without that cringe of embarrassment that holds you back from launching into a strange language. I talked to a friend recently about his attempt to learn French as a mature student. Like me he found the written work comparatively easy but it was torture to try and answer a question in French in front of anyone, including his teacher.

I now have lists of words, nouns, verbs, adverbs and adjectives. Grace encourages me to use them as building blocks for sentences, nuggets of speech that I might use in real life. I can invite someone to an Internet café, tell them that I'm going to the supermarket, or order a beer. I can write a strange stilted story about myself in the third person. Kai se Lin is a student. She goes to Merrion Square university. Deng Xiao e is her teacher. She watches television. She listens to the radio. She studies Chinese. She is not very busy today. Tomorrow she will be very busy.

Day Eleven

A Friday lesson. It's a relief to get to the end of the week. In China you are not likely to have a conversation centring around the weather as you would in Ireland. Food and tea are much more common topics of small talk. The rough translation of weather is *tian qi* but the words mean more than just weather. *Tian* (which can also mean day) here means the sky and *qi* is loosely translated as energy. It's an idea of weather as nature, an absolute power, the air around us and the energy in which we all exist.

The word for stuff is *dong xi*, which literally translates as 'east west'. *Bei* is 'north', giving us Beijing, the north capital. Tokyo is Dongjing, the eastern capital. There is no word in Chinese for the western capital.

Respect for age is a large part of the language, with different ways to ask someone their age. You can simply ask a child, 'you, what age?' but this would be 'very offensive' to an older person. Between teenage years and the thirties you ask someone *duo da* or 'how big?'

Anyone older than thirty is asked their age with four words *duo da nian ling*, which literally translates as 'how big year age?'

I'm enjoying writing my lists of words, memorising them and trying to repeat them back to myself with one hand covering the answers. It's a satisfying thing to do. I'm also enjoying the prospect of a weekend off from classes.

Day Fourteen

'Are you married?' and 'Do you have children?' are typical conversation openers in China. This is not, as would be the case in Ireland, followed by 'How many children do you have?' Because of the one child policy having children means having one child, not several.

Words that have had to be invented to deal with modern life have a meaning of their own in Chinese. A computer is a *dian nao*, *dian* meaning 'electric' and *nao* meaning 'brains'. So your laptop or PC is your electric brain, which goes back to the idea of outsourcing our brain's work to computers. Similarly, a television is an electric image, a film an electric shadow. A cell phone is a *shou ji* or hand machine.

My tin ear for the spoken language seems to be getting worse. Grace can ask me very simple questions using words I have spoken and written and I won't understand them until I take what she says and try to repeat it back to myself out loud, slowly. I haven't had a breakthrough moment where the switch in my brain clicks and I can understand Mandarin spoken with any speed or complexity. I console myself with the Chinesepod sessions, testing myself by playing the dialogue and trying to understand it before it is broken down and explained by the ever chirpy Ken and his female assistant.

Over the weekend my Chinese homework folder remained resolutely closed. I'm playing catchup again this Monday morning and other work is pressing in on the time I have to sit and bend my head around this language.

Day Fifteen

It is becoming a process of turning these strange new words into my own possessions, components that I can reach for when I need to form a sentence. We are back to Ebbinghaus's 'possessions of the soul' and my soul is a long way from owning any great knowledge of Mandarin. But I'm finding the process of trying very interesting.

Today has been particularly fraught, not helped by the fact that I'm feeling tired from daily classes. When I open my folder to revise I am ragged round the edges. But soon, in the company of that morning's words, trying to put them into sentences and speak them out loud in the quiet of the kitchen, I feel calmer. There is something meditative about learning. It switches off the buzzing thoughts of tasks yet to do or situations where I felt I could have done better or that negative niggling voice that sets itself off when I'm feeling tired and defeated. When I'm repeating Chinese nouns to myself and trying to get myself to remember that adding the word *le* puts a sentence into the past tense or that the word for 'not' changes from *bu* to *mei* depending on the tense, the inner voice shuts up and listens.

Day Seventeen

The kitchen table is where I sit to do my Chinese homework. I could take it into the spare bedroom where my desk and computer sit but it feels better to work on this in a different place. I am away from the screen and in a different zone.

Yesterday I had no class and had promised myself that I would sit at the kitchen table for an hour and work as if I were in the classroom. I managed about twenty minutes before I got up to do something else, then closed the folder entirely. Without the structure of a class my resolution to do this for a set amount of time each day dissolves easily. The kettle calls to me from across the room to make some tea (which in fact is eminently a part of Chinese culture). Grace carries a flask of tea to each class. Most Chinese people spend all day drinking tea, she explains. When she first arrived in Ireland with her Irish husband she found the tea bag tea with sugar and milk in it one of the biggest culture shocks. In China you would be served tea made from tea bags only in the cheapest of hostels. And it is never served with milk or sugar, despite the national sweet tooth that sees many Chinese people diluting red wine with cola.

This morning we have an earlier lesson as I have a meeting at the time we would normally meet. It feels good to get the work done earlier and again my brain feels more refreshed and ready to learn. That night I go to the opening of Colm Tóibín's *Testament*, his first stage play. Tóibín sits two rows in front of me watching intently, perched on the edge of his seat as if ready to flee the building. Marie Mullen performs the one woman show with a ferocious strength and power, telling the story of the life of Jesus from the point of view of his mother Mary. It is an angry, dense and bleak script and it is an extraordinary feat of memory to unspool those thousands of words on stage, turning the bland wallpaper crucifixion scene we all know from Christian childhood stories into a visceral witness statement.

Day Eighteen

Another early morning class and because it's Friday I'm exhausted by the end of it. We are covering time telling and shopping, using the Chinese currency RMB or *ren min bi*, which translates as 'the people's collective money'. Confusingly, there are both official and unofficial terms for units of currency (similar to our old 'pound' and 'quid'). The main unit is the *yuan* but it is also called the *kuai*, the next unit down (a tenth of a *yuan*) is the *jiao*, which is also called the *mao*, and finally there is the penny unit or *fen* which is known by only one name.

I'm finding it helpful to revise by going back to my notes on the first days' lessons. Otherwise I find that the words I learned then are slipping away under the weight of the new information that's coming with every lesson. Again it strikes me that living in a Chinese speaking world would help to prevent this. Rehearsing simple social speech and hearing it every day is the only way to get things to stick.

I summon the courage to try my Chinese with Shirley, a teacher at the yoga studio. '*Ni shi hen hao laoshi*,' I say to her as I'm leaving after her class. 'You are very good teacher.'

She's delighted and very encouraging of my efforts. She warns against picking up a bad Chinese accent. She has a friend who speaks in an accent she finds rough and grating. She winces when she describes it, then smiles her beautiful smile.

Day Twenty Two

It has taken twenty days to get to what is often the first word of a new language that people learn: 'Cheers'. Chinese people say *gan bei*, literally translated as 'empty cup', an exhortation to down your drink in one swallow.

For tonight's homework I fill a foolscap page with columns of words, the verbs, adjectives and nouns and general expressions (like 'I'm sorry' or 'excuse me') that I have been learning. Then I fill another page with sentences using some of these words.

The more time I spend in the evenings refreshing what I've learned that morning the easier it is to open the folder the next day and start where I left off. Trying to learn a language, like any physical challenge, is easiest when you do a little every day. And motivation comes from doing. I do feel my energy levelling off from the initial burst. As the ideas and sentences become more complex this is becoming more tiring. The lessons and homework are eating up all the spare minutes I have. There is no time to listen to Chinese language downloads, practise speaking the words or train my ear to recognise them.

Day Twenty Two

The idea of the measure word becomes clearer today. It differentiates between a phrase that means five months and the very similar phrase that means May, or the fifth month. Five months has the measure word *ge* in it to indicate that you are talking about a quantity of time.

Many words are repeated for emphasis in informal speech. In a kind of Mrs Doyle ism of 'go on, go on, go on,' a Chinese person might urge you to taste something by saying 'taste taste', *chang yi chang*. 'Wait', 'listen', 'watch' can similarly be doubled for emphasis.

Day Twenty Five

At the end of my last full week of Chinese I collapse gratefully into the company of close friends on the Friday evening to celebrate two birthdays that fall close together. It's been a hectic few months and I can feel my resources and enthusiasm waning. Life is busy for everyone and we rarely have the chance to get together like this.

Although no one had an inkling of it then, in just over two months one of our group would be gone, suddenly, shockingly, with her voice and smile and personality like a long deep note resonating through everyone's life in the following months. Although it wasn't the last time I saw Maria – I would see her twice more – that night goes down as a last moment of innocence; a time when I had a childlike trust in some kind of karmic order or fairness, that good things happen to good people.

Day Thirty

There's been a trip to Galway, a breakneck dash back to Dublin to make a friend's fortieth brunch and several other reasons not to open my Chinese homework. Today I finish with a double class, to make up for missing the day before.

Although I'm still in Merrion Square, where the canopy of trees has turned from late summer green to browns and yellows and russets, we get into a Beijing taxi for the last test. It's a dialogue between the driver and a visiting Irish person. The driver is an inquisitive type who wants to know everything about his passenger. He compliments the passenger's Chinese as being very good. 'It's so so,' I answer as the passenger. Here Grace gives me the equivalent phrase in Chinese. To say that you are 'so so' at something, you say 'horse, horse, tiger, tiger'. I love this phrase. It sums up exactly where I've got to with most of the challenges in this book. Some days my abilities as a gardener, flute player, runner, yoga practitioner or whatever are just like a horse, an old plodding dray horse who's tired of pulling his cart. But there are momentary glimpses of an orange and black striped flank, dimly through the jungle.

6

Maria

Maria Ruane doesn't belong in this book. If life was fair she would be in a warm slant of sunshine in a coffee shop reading it, through the steam of a great cappuccino.

Maria fizzed with energy. She arrived like a detonation of good humour into your house. Grinning and talking, she would peer over the cook's shoulder, taste whatever was to hand, then launch into a story or a funny account of some incident. If you arrived at her busy, bustling house you pulled up a stool and got fed. More often than not someone else's child or dog was there. Things would often be so busy you might have to put the kettle on yourself to make tea but that was fine.

On a Friday morning in December 2011 we talked on the phone. I sat in a chair in my quiet, empty kitchen for a good long chat. Mercifully there was no computer screen in front of me to soak up half my attention. She was happy, tired and not feeling well, but contented. She talked about how great her kids were: her eldest Sean (15), who had been looking after her when she was sick in bed, the unstoppable Catherine (12) and her talents and projects and the lovely Maeve (8) whom she'd been worried about because she'd been sick. 'Take care and mind yourself,' I think I said before hanging up. I went back upstairs and continued working at my desk. I will always regret not getting into the car and going to see her that day.

Later that night the book club we were part of met for Christmas drinks. Someone texted her to say they were raising a glass to her. 'As long as it's flat 7 Up,' she texted back.

Two days later Maria was catastrophically ill, on a life support system. The sickness that had her in bed was not a bad winter bug but a viciously aggressive form of leukaemia. An oncologist would later describe it as a runaway train. By the time she got the diagnosis the cancer was in its final stages. They switched off the machines on the Monday morning, just over sixty hours after we had spoken on the phone. My funny, wise and beautiful friend died with her parents and her husband Mark at her bedside. It was thirteen days to Christmas.

Maria had joked about this book project. A gifted clown, she mimed my manic schedule, her fingers flashing from tootling an invisible flute to digging an allotment to eating the dinners I was paid to review. It was typical Maria, poking gentle fun at a friend who was often in danger of taking herself far too seriously.

Yet she was a living example of what it was I was trying to do, with my manic schedule of flute lessons and late night gardening. In the last year of her life she revelled in being alive. She would describe a stunning sky as she cycled across the city to work, how she had to read a profoundly beautiful sentence in a book twice just to savour it; the first sip of a cup of coffee with no one to interrupt her, a song or a piece of music she luxuriated in for a few snatched minutes. She had a gift for living. And in her work as a psychologist working with young people she knew how important it was to live in the moment. She knew the value of the now, how it could heal a troubled mind and be a deep and constantly available source of peace.

Death reduces even the most vibrant people to threadbare clichés. Describing Maria as a brilliant mother, friend, wife and daughter reduces her to plaster saint. And she was never that. She was much too honest to pretend that life was easy. Growing up without sisters, I replaced them with female friends. She was one of that small tight circle of sisters. She inspired me to try to have a home birth with my first pregnancy and trust my instincts with my terrifying new baby who was born ten days before her youngest daughter. She was fiercely strong and capable, a person who took a problem and broke it down into a process, the end of which would provide a solution. Had she been given the chance she would have dealt with serious illness in the same way.

My loss is a fraction of that felt by her family. Yet my home is full of emotional land mines, things she gave me over the years, like the pair of mittens my youngest son wears with her family name written in her hand on the label inside. I live in fear of losing them because it would be a loss of one more connection to her. In the aftermath of her death I struggled to see a point in anything. I was gripped by a feeling of urgency and preciousness about the time we are given, guilty that I was still around to enjoy the world and angry and impatient with the national spirit of despondency that oozed from the airwaves.

In the allotment the mint and horseradish plants she gave me, with the warning that I shouldn't plant them in open ground, are thriving, growing and spreading just as she warned. I can hear her voice saying, 'Jaysus, you shoulda listened to me.' Weeks after she died, a dusty, forgotten picture frame with three shots in it stopped me in my tracks. The first shows me smiling from a swing on a warm summer's day, the second my eldest boy, still a baby, in another swing and the third shows Maria's son Sean looking levelly at the camera with his mother's calm brown eyes. She took the photographs. We were all looking at her. And we were all happy, caught in a simple moment of play in her back garden.

At her funeral Mass her husband Mark talked about his road map for the years ahead. 'What would Maria do?' would be the question he would ask at every turn, he said.

One of the things Maria would do would be to look for a moment every day, fleeting or longer, when she felt fully alive, a 'self actualisation' moment, to use the psychological term. And those calming touchstones came from simple things. She is there with me in those moments when I take a deep breath and remember to stop and try just to be. She is the companion of my solitary coffee shop visits. I can still hear her voice and her laughter. Her death taught me to value the sense of potential in the ordinary everyday world and to see life as an adventure into which we must welcome fun and hope at every opportunity.

7

Bake

Everything to this point had been about me. I was entirely self absorbed. My schedule read like that of a pampered Brooklyn brat shuttling from a flute lesson to a Mandarin class. Maria's death jolted me out of that bubble. I wanted to make the final task centre around doing something for others.

People with time on their hands often find it difficult to pitch in, roll up their sleeves and get involved in some kind of community effort. They may be too shy to push themselves forward at a residents' meeting, or have lived too busy a life to make those connections in their communities that can lead to helping out and getting involved. Often, community organisations appear to be staffed by tightly knit groups of people who don't seem particularly open to new arrivals. We blow ins may be viewed suspiciously as people who will dabble a bit, then leave.

Organisations like Volunteer Ireland have been set up to match people with time and skills to those who need them. It's becoming easier to find a place to welcome you with open arms. For a few weeks I hoped to be able to bake bread in Crumlin Children's Hospital. I had landed in the A&E department of this crumbling place during the summer when my middle son accidentally poked his younger brother in the eye with a stick. Thankfully he was fine but we sat in their waiting room for hours waiting to be seen. There was nothing available to eat but vending machine junk and the usual cellophane wrapped processed food in the hospital café. I sent an angry tweet out bemoaning the situation and the hospital's research arm contacted me to say they had just installed a new kitchen. They were interested, they said, in getting chefs involved in trying to improve the food.

I sent out a general appeal for someone to help and restaurateur Ronan Ryan got in touch. Along with the nutrition expert Susan Jane White, we put together a ten point plan to improve things, none of which would cost the hospital money. In fact, it had the potential to save money from the catering budget, using fresh ingredients and setting up a *stage* or work experience system for young catering graduates. I offered to come and bake bread every day for thirty days and we had provisional agreement from organic flour providers Ballybrado to supply the ingredients. The people from the research and fundraising arm of the hospital were very enthusiastic but the plan had to go to the powers that be. Then it withered slowly in that typical Irish fashion where instead of saying 'no' they just said nothing. In a follow up query I asked why the plan had met with no response and in response I got another long, deep email silence. Months later I decided I had to find another endeavour: I would donate whatever I made to a leukaemia charity.

The idea of making something by hand, like daily baking, appealed to me. So I decided to bake.

Baking is back. It's one of the stories of the moment. The heroine in the film *Bridesmaids* is a cake baker; author Marian Keyes has just published a book called *Saved By Cake* about how baking helped her fight depression; *The Great British Bake Off* was a surprise ratings hit on the BBC.

How often do we read about a high flying executive/architect/ management consultant who turns his or her kitchen skills into a business? We know the narrative and it's always threaded through with emotion, much more love than you'll find in interviews with cost accountants or chartered surveyors. I've rarely interviewed anyone about a food enterprise without the 'p' word coming into it. That's 'p' for passion, rather than 'p' for profit. It seems that people work in food for the love of what they do. Food producers are still some of the most positive people you will find even in recession ridden Ireland, so it's not surprising that baking features so strongly in people's alternative dream job list.

I already knew how to bake. But could I bake something unique and sell it to people? Could I make money as a food producer and would I find that underneath all the talk about love and passion there are long lonely hours of hard manual labour?

'Unpromising' doesn't begin to describe my first efforts. On the first day I spent an hour in the kitchen, after which I had a tray of buns that look like spoonfuls of soil covered in gobs of spit.

The spit soil muffins were the first of my experiments in baking with a difference, a niche into which I could sell my idea as well as my product. I was trying to devise a tasty sugar free treat. It seemed to be an under exploited area: most home baked cakes and buns are loaded with sugar.

As soon as I started to experiment in the kitchen I could see exactly why. Sugar is cheap and it makes things taste great. My spit muffins were made with stevia, a sugar substitute that comes from the herb of that name. It's the latest in sugar alternatives to be found in the supermarket aisle. In my research on stevia it sounded like a miracle ingredient, super sweet so you only need a little, natural and without the blood sugar spike you get from sucrose.

Then I bought it. A branded sweetener version (mixed with the bulking agent Malodextrin) it came in a white box that weighed as if it was stuffed with goose down and cost nearly €6. I wanted to try chocolate brownies. I opened the stevia box and found a dazzling white powder inside. Taking a teaspoon out, I instantly missed the weight of sugar, that heaviness that tells you it's going to melt and caramelise and do all those other luscious things that sugar does. This was more like powdered polystyrene, flyaway and fake looking. It tasted strangely bitter and too sweet at the same time and left a nasty synthetic aftertaste. But I ploughed on.

The brownie mixture – made with pure cacao and melted butter, ground almonds, eggs, vanilla extract and stevia – did not look promising. But what brownie mix does? This is one of the magic things about cake. You put something lumpy and liquid in the oven and the alchemy of baking makes it rise, turning it into a smooth fluffy sponge, with a firm top which might crack to reveal softer layers beneath.

None of this happened here. It was weird. After cooking, the mixture was in exactly the same state as when I had spooned it into the bun cases, rough and lumpy like soil. I closed the oven and hoped this was just the first stage. But there was worse to come. Towards the end of the cooking time the brown lumps started to ooze liquid that looked like spit bubbles at the edges.

Then they were cooked. The raw mixture had tasted bad enough. The cooked versions made you want to claw the food out of your mouth and rinse with something strong. Stevia and bitter cacao had made a brownie so bitter it could stage its own one man show on the state of the economy.

Day Two

'Those are the best buns I've ever tasted,' was the enthusiastic feedback from a visiting five year old to a traditional bun recipe with ground almonds, clementine zest and a modest amount of sugar.

I needed to pitch my product somewhere between the vile mouthfuls of my first experiment and the yummy treats of the traditional sugary buns. Years ago I had rediscovered the joy of a traditional Irish tea brack, raisins and sultanas soaked overnight in strong brown tea, then stirred with eggs, flour, some spices and a little sugar into a moist, fruit laden cake, perfect slathered with butter and eaten with a cup of tea. I had already tweaked the recipe by using date syrup instead of sugar. It worked well, much of the sweetness coming from the swollen dried fruit that complemented the date syrup. But tea brack buns weren't such a success. The trick was the spreading of butter and you couldn't slather butter on to a muffin.

Day Three

I am married to a sugar fiend. So when he said 'yum' to a mouthful of sugar free granola bars I began to think this might work. The Internet is a world of ideas and recipes for every kind of cooking you can imagine. If Mrs Beeton was alive today she'd be a food blogger, cutting and pasting recipes and ideas just as she did by hand for her *Book of Household Management* in the 19th century, then making them her own by delivering them in her distinctive, bossy Victorian voice. Modern cooks have millions of ideas through which they can browse for inspiration every day. I found a sugar free granola bar recipe online, sweetened with mashed bananas and dried fruit, so nothing synthetic or whiter than white.

The mixture of fruit, seeds, nuts and oat flakes was bound together with a warmed cashew butter and mashed bananas, spread on a baking sheet and baked in the oven. It cut pretty well into bars, then became not quite snap crisp (the other thing sugar does) but not too bendy either.

So maybe I'd found a recipe? But something niggled about the granola bars. They were too predictable and also very health foody. Yes you could pitch them as a breakfast bar for people too time pressed for a bowl of porridge, or a 3pm slump bar full of healthy slow release energy. But would you yearn for one with a cup of coffee? Probably not.

Day Four and On…

I got the flu. The real thing, the lie in bed can't do anything dose. This was a severe setback. Days passed in a blur of sleeping and grumbling. I couldn't look at food. Every time I appeared downstairs my sons cheered at the resumption of normality. Then I would have to head back up the stairs and lie down again.

The aftermath of the flu was both physical and mental. My motivation dwindled and petered out like a spent match. It was as if someone had left a tap running so the reserves of energy that I could dip into on busier days had gone. I couldn't run, cycle or walk much, so my mood dipped further. The drive to get this last project off the ground was gone. The irony wasn't lost on me. Here I was writing a book about using every day and days were passing when getting dressed before midday was my sole achievement.

I reread the expert advice, the simple idea that motivation comes from doing and that it's easier to do a lot over a long time by doing a little every day. The words did little to get my cotton wool brain moving. Sitting down at the keyboard to write and research was becoming impossible. My kite brain flitted from Twitter to email and browsing favourite websites. I bought a truly ugly coat online because it was cheap.

The Buddhist 'this too will pass' phrase popped into my head. This drop in energy and morale was probably a consequence of cramming so much into the months gone by. It was also a physical reaction to the death of a close friend. Fatigue is not one of the better known stages of grief but another friend described feeling tired for a year after her mother died.

Day Twelve

I am back on my feet and across a desk from Susan Richardson, a woman who has a gut feeling for an idea that will work. She's seen people like me who want to be food producers sit in her office and pitch their idea, often with a plate of food on the table. As the manager of the Spade Enterprise Centre in North King Street in Dublin she is the woman people come to when they've been cooking in their own kitchens for the farmers' markets or stalls and want to grow bigger.

The Spade Centre has nineteen catering kitchens of different sizes that can be hired on a monthly basis. If I were doing my baking project for real I would be presenting my business plan, information about me and my product and pitching it all to Susan and her board. The smallest kitchens cost around €400 a month, plus VAT and energy bills. The largest ones are up to €2,000 a month. The real attraction for a start up is that the tenancy can be terminated with one month's notice. You also find yourself in a supportive community of other startups with help and advice on hand if you hit an obstacle.

The longest part of the process of setting up a food operation is getting the all clear from the environmental health officers who have to certify that everything is being done to minimum food safety standards. Anything involving raw meat is extremely complicated.

Housed in a converted church, the Spade Centre has been providing workshop, kitchen and office space for startup businesses since 1990. They could get someone up and running in a new kitchen in a month but it would probably take longer to have food safety approval in place.

'When people come in here they are usually very enthusiastic.

They have a real chin up attitude,' Susan says. 'You can sense their enthusiasm from the minute they call.'

She judges them not only on their product but on their ability to work hard. 'In the first year you see people going non stop. There's the fear of failure so they put body and soul, blood sweat and tears into it.' She advises anyone starting off to get a good accounts package to keep track of who owes you money and to whom you owe money. Often new businesses are thrown when an invoice they were counting on doesn't get paid on time. 'That knocks the stuffing out of them and can be a bit of a shock,' she says. 'Then sometimes the products they think are going to move well don't and they have to rethink things.'

It's here that the 'passion' of being a food producer meets the reality of running a food business. Figuring out accountancy software, distribution or packing logistics is never going to be as enjoyable as stirring melting chocolate into a ganache. But without the business brain the best food producer will find getting their products out to lots of customers next to impossible.

Caoimhe Smyth has just taken a unit in the Spade Centre, making grain free bread. She had been baking at home and selling in farmers' markets and has now moved into supplying shops and small supermarkets. Her Primal Breads are handmade from a variety of non grain flours, such as nut flours. It's low carb and high protein bread so it suits not just the coeliac market but the energy food market for people training or doing intensive exercise.

She has found the process of setting up a business one of 'constantly learning on your feet'. There is so much to learn every day and her evenings are spent in her office (which is also her bedroom) managing the business end of the venture. 'I'm up till all hours. You're really a one man band, full time sales as well as manufacturing. I'm exhausted but still happy that this is the path I'm on.'

She is now moving into crackers and plans to start making cakes soon. Her unit is the size of a largish living room, pristinely clean and orderly. She wears heavy cotton chef's whites, an apron over them and a small white hat to keep her hair up.

She found the experience of selling at her market stall a great starting point. 'People are very honest face to face.' And she learned not to take criticism personally. 'You have to let go of a massive amount. It's a passion, but you need to make money.'

Day Thirteen

Chocolate. The word is enough to make people melt at the edges. It is a high pleasure food, one of life's great things. I'm adding small pieces of butter into a bowl of warm, dark, thick chocolatey sauce. Each yellow cube is swallowed by the dark brown mixture and melts slowly into it, turning it slightly more smooth and glossy with each stir. This is a ganache, or thick chocolate topping, made with warmed cream, maple syrup, raw cacao, then those pieces of butter added at the end. When it's still warm it has the consistency of thick pouring cream. It cools to a soft buttery fudge consistency.

I think I may have found my product. I'm pouring the ganache on top of a dark brown chocolate bun. The maple syrup and cacao have combined to give it an almost caramel flavour. No one can call these buns health food. Cream and butter are a major part of the ingredients. The sweetener in the bun itself is agave syrup, a refined syrup from a Mexican cactus plant. Agave, a fructose rather than a sucrose, has become a staple health shop alternative to refined sugar. And it is expensive, roughly ten times the cost of sugar.

Doing the maths on cupcakes I can see why they have become such a staple in baking repertoires. Were I to make these buns with cheap sugar and cheap chocolate the cost of the raw ingredients that goes into them would be around thirty cent per cupcake, not factoring in any major bulk discounts for ingredients, which could bring the cost down even further. At a modest sale price of €2.50 it's a mark up of 87 per cent. Of course labour and equipment costs would also have to be factored in but cupcakes are a seam of gold if you're producing them in large quantities and selling them directly to your customer.

Like novelty cakes they're made to beguile the eye. Cupcakes are jazz hands. Cupcakes are fun. The cake element itself is largely irrelevant, a blank canvas for drawing swirls of icing. The average child will eat a cupcake by pushing it into their face top side first and using their tongue to lick all the icing off. The bun is often discarded like a used ice lolly stick. No one worries that the bun is probably as tasty as sawdust. It's all about the topping, the butter cream icing topped with another sugar laced decoration. Many of them look as if they've been designed by sugar crazed children let loose in a sweet shop.

Day Fourteen

I once asked Anthony Bourdain why people were so fascinated by chefs. The famous American TV personality, who made his fortune from writing about the real people in kitchens, looked stumped for a second. We were sitting in the RTÉ canteen, minutes before he went on air to talk about *Medium Raw*, his second volume of memoirs, a follow up to his million selling restaurant insider cook and tell book, *Kitchen Confidential*. 'I've discussed this with chefs many times,' he said. 'In our private moments we're baffled by it. We're so used to being marginal characters on the fringe of society. To suddenly be the focus of attention is still baffling. Something happened.'

My theory is that, caught between celebrity culture and a growing sense of alienation, people became hungry for a connection with real things, so now food and the stories of the people who cook or produce it are at the centre of things. Because so many of us make so little with our hands we are slightly in awe of those who do. I suspect a large segment of the food and cooking television show audience have just put a pre prepared meal in the oven to free them up to watch their cookery show. Real food, the home made stew or home peeled and mashed buttery spuds, is becoming like porn: it's something you watch. In celebrating people who make things with their hands, we've chosen to idolise the chefs, not the joiners or the jewellers. Charisma is key. Heaven knows how the scientists seeking a cure for cancer feel about it all.

A chef's celebrity status can shift more produce than his or her skill in the kitchen. Selling cookbooks can be much more lucrative (and much less hard work) than sautéing scallops for fifty diners. The chefs who quietly cook, doing their own thing their own way, are pushed aside in the rush to celebrity. My bookshelves are stacked with expensive cookbooks, many of which lie unopened, most of which promise something more than just a tasty meal, a return to some kind of human connection to things that are real and worthwhile. Food has become an accessory, a class statement, part of the that awful world of 'lifestyle' that can often be devoid of both life and style.

Day Fifteen

'What's that?' my two year old shrieked when I went to pick him up from playschool. He was talking about my black trouser suit, which I'd felt compelled to don as a sort of armour to combat the nerves of my first taste test for the cupcakes. He had never seen me wearing a suit. Until this stereotype shattering moment suits were something his dad wore to work.

The suit was designed to bolster my courage as I brought four chocolate cupcakes for a taste test to my first customers, a new café and interiors shop called Union Square in Terenure. If I were doing this for real I would probably go about getting a market stall or stalls, selling directly to the public for the highest price I could pitch. But selling them through an existing food business would speed things up. A market pitch could take weeks to organise. Most of the best ones have long waiting lists of people who want to sell at them.

Going this route meant skipping the customer interaction from which small producers get so much valuable feedback, not to mention a warm glow. People shop in farmers' markets in a different way from their harried supermarket trip. They stroll and taste and smile and relax. A trip to the market is seen by some people as a pleasant way to spend time rather than a strip lit half hour of torture to a sound track of supermarket musack and tannoy announcements.

In the end the suit wasn't necessary. The owners of Union Square had a quick taste and liked them. Three of the four were left behind and vanished quickly from the plate, nibbled in between one service and the next in the kitchen. This seemed like a good omen.

I spent the next ten days baking batches of the buns, ordering ingredients and trying to get my head around the food safety regulations.

Day Twenty Five

HACCP, or 'Hassip' as it's pronounced by the people who use it, was developed by NASA for astronauts in the 1960s to produce food that could be safely eaten in space. That's the most exciting thing about it. The acronym stands for Hazard Analysis and Critical Control Point, so it's about keeping meticulous records of points at which food might be contaminated. That means recording fridge temperatures, core temperatures, delivery batch numbers, time and place of cooking and probe thermometer readings.

An ideal way to produce food, in the eyes of a food safety expert, would be in a sterile unit staffed by robots, coated in an antibacterial substance, a clean room into which none of the bags of swill laden with bacteria that are human beings would be permitted.

To a food safety expert, humans ooze potentially dangerous bacteria from every orifice. Even before we think about bathroom habits they shed hairs, skin cells, sweat and mucus. Then there's the human urge to scratch, pick, rub or otherwise contaminate ourselves and our surroundings. All this can contaminate the food we are working with, passing on bacteria that could cause an outbreak of food borne illness.

In the 1960s the World Health Organisation took HACCP on board and in the 1990s it became law in European countries.

Many food producers see HACCP as the enemy of taste: flavour dimmed by refrigeration, over cooking (a medium raw burger is forbidden under HACCP rules) and paranoia about bacteria. On the other hand the rules ensure that food sold to the public is produced in clean kitchens by people who wash their hands and wear hairnets and ensure that batches of food on their watch are made as safely as possible.

In order to cook for the public I have to learn about HACCP. The Food Safety Authority of Ireland have a pack, including a DVD, food record sheets and easy instructions. At €70 it's not inexpensive but it gives me the basics.

Under HACCP I have to buy my raw ingredients from reputable suppliers and record where every ingredient came from and the date of its delivery. I have to record the length of cooking times, the temperatures and how quickly things were put into the fridge. It's a long way from the romance or even the passion of creating food. But it's part of the picture if you want to go from cooking for friends and family to cooking for the wider public.

The presence of our small adored dog in our house means that I can't bake my cupcakes at home. I will have to find a professional kitchen.

And I will have to buy a hairnet.

Day Twenty Six

By now I could bake these buns in my sleep. It's a simple recipe and it's quick (up to a point). Everything is put into the food processor, whizzed into a smooth batter and poured into paper cases. I have cooked batch after batch of these and think I've got the flavour correct. I'm using a very expensive raw cacao for the ganache as the cheaper one makes it taste too bitter. It means that any mistake in a batch of ganache is going to be expensive. I make one batch with some heavy cream I haven't used before and it turns out odd, the fudge icing breaking up slightly as I pipe it, rather than going on smoothly.

I have an apron, a hairnet and two large boxes of supplies. The two litre milk carton has been stored in the fridge with a label on it (*for the cupcakes – keep off!*) so it doesn't get poured on the morning porridge by mistake.

Cookery writer, Domini Kemp, my colleague in *The Irish Times* magazine, is one of Ireland's top food entrepreneurs. She runs the Itsa chain of bagel shops and cafes with her sister, Peaches. When I asked her for advice about finding a professional kitchen she kindly offered me a stint in the Itsa catering kitchen.

Her chef, Philip Thomas, scanned the recipe when I went to talk about the logistics. He'd used the Willie's Supreme Raw Cacao I was using in the ganache to make a traditional south American hot chocolate, just cacao grated into boiling water. It was nothing like our idea of hot chocolate, milky and sweet, but black and intense, more like a strong jolt of coffee. They had been experimenting with some sugar free recipes, the latest substitute being an apple and grape syrup. Some of the products sold well but only when they were put on special offer.

I was beginning to wonder if I were trying to straddle two markets and would fall between the two. People who were interested in sugar free food were probably not going to be as tempted by a chocolate cupcake as a more healthy looking treat. Someone who wanted a cupcake might not want it to be sugar free.

Day Twenty Eight

This was the land of the giants. In the Itsa kitchen everything was as you might find it in a well equipped domestic kitchen, only bigger and in multiple quantities. Wooden spoons, spatulas and whisks had extra long handles, big enough to scoop large quantities of cake mixture out of the enormous stainless steel bowls. Measuring jugs were over a foot tall. The ovens could take rack after rack of trays and the heat they blasted out would cook things way faster than any domestic oven. My 'station' was in the pastry area with its granite worktop (which I assume was cold for rolling pastry). I went for the smaller mixer: a larger one was a bit too like a cement mixer. I hefted in my boxes of ingredients and went to get changed into a chef's jacket, apron, hairnet and hairband.

I'd left all my jewellery at home, rings threaded on to a bracelet to keep them safe. My nails were short and scrubbed.

It's difficult to pull a heavy cotton chef's jacket over your head and not imagine yourself in an episode of *Masterchef.* The long sleeved top had a snap button at the neck and I tied my stiff new apron around the front. People working in kitchens move quickly and efficiently. As I followed Cáit Griffith, the pastry chef, around to find equipment I found myself getting in the way when she turned quickly to come back to the pastry area. She was more than patient with the newbie in her kitchen.

I had a gleaming work station and all the equipment I needed. I had my bearings and it was time to start to bake. I was going to make the buns in batches of twenty four. The plan was to make seventy, thirty for the new Itsa café in Ranelagh, twenty four for Union Square and the rest for others who had helped. I'd multiplied quantities but soon found myself short of bun batter. A new tray had wider bun slots so each cupcake was taking more batter than usual. The buns themselves looked more like wide splats than the taller narrow ones I'd been making in the other tray. I put them in the oven and Cait recommended twelve minutes cooking time. At home in my fan oven they would take up to twenty five minutes.

After six minutes they didn't seem to be rising. I could feel myself fretting. Would I have to bin the first batch and start again? Watched cupcakes don't rise so I got on with the ganache. At a huge hob I stirred a large batch of cream and maple syrup together. The mixture turned to a caramel colour and smelled delicious. I turned the heat off and in went around €14 worth of the expensive raw cacao. It melted quickly into the mixture, turning it instantly dark. Over a tiny flame I started stirring in more than 700g of butter, a chunk at a time. It seemed to take for ever. I knew that if I didn't let each chunk melt completely before adding the next I ran the risk of a small piece of unmelted butter turning up in the icing. There was no shortcut here. Melting the butter separately would just make the mixture split and curdle. There was nothing for it but to stand and stir, patiently. After years of writing about the merits of slow food, here I was, peppering to hurry up a process that would make this icing taste better.

The first batch of buns was baked and cooling. They had risen well. Cait helped me with toasted hazelnuts, rubbing the papery brown skins off them after they were toasted, then blitzing them to a powder and small chunk consistency. These were going to be sprinkled over the icing after I had piped it on. They smelled gorgeous.

A blast freezer cooled the buns straight out of the oven in minutes and also cooled the icing to its fudge consistency. It highlighted the merits of a fully equipped kitchen for saving time. It might have taken years of working at markets and small producer level to be able to invest in this equipment for my own business.

Then came the fun bit. By now the kitchen had emptied and, probably for the first time all day, it was calm and quiet. I had a large piping bag and I was putting swirls of icing on the buns with a big nozzle. It was a simple circle closing in on itself. The pinch off at the end was not always perfectly centred so a sprinkle of the toasted hazelnuts was very forgiving of any wobbles. By then I had sixty nine buns in polka dot cases with a swirl of chocolate icing and dusted with the yellow toasted nuts. The seventieth was tested by Cait. She said she liked it a lot. I was chuffed. A professional pastry chef knows her buns.

I packed them into boxes and put them into the walk in fridge, a massive chilled room with white shelves. I made the rookie mistake of trying to walk through the heavy plastic curtains tray first. Jack, a young chef finishing his shift, came to help move them before they knocked all my hard work to the floor. The next time I walked in back first, holding my precious buns out in front of me.

It had taken slightly more than three hours to make the batch of buns. My legs were aching and I was exhausted. I spritzed and cleaned down my work station, put on the alarm, locked up and pulled the shutter down over the heavy metal door.

Day Twenty Nine

Kevin Byrne felt strangely sad when he saw the six tables being unloaded from the van and carried inside. The sturdy secondhand restaurant tables were perfect for his latest venture, a new café in Terenure, to be called Union Square. But Kevin knew these tables intimately. As a sixteen year old he had wiped them down many times during his shifts at the cheap and cheerful city centre restaurant where hordes of hungry people had eaten over the years. That place had closed and the tables were now his.

Just two years earlier he and his partner took the leap of faith to open up 'their own place'. The move came after long years of working for people in other restaurants. Before they went into business together, both Kevins were comfortably ensconced in jobs, one as manager of Avoca's Fernhouse Restaurant in Kilmacanogue, the other as head chef in the Canal Bank Café on Leeson Street.

The drive to move out of that comfort zone and open their own place came to a head one day after a visit to a friend, Caroline, and Nelly's, her lovely café on the South Circular Road. Driving home they saw a 'shop to let' sign in an old butcher's in Terenure that they had always wondered about. It was tiny and there was nowhere to park outside. The dark green and gold painted exterior made it virtually invisible to the passerby. Inside the old tiles were cracked and old meat racks still hung from the ceiling.

Kevin the chef cashed in his SSIA money and they took out a credit union loan and begged, borrowed and stole furniture to put it all together. They called their tiny new neighbourhood café Mayfield Deli and Eatery. In the end they left the meat racks and the cracked tiles of the old interior, the character and history of the place growing on them as they stood there wondering how to make it work. Now they employ fourteen people.

Front of house Kevin remembers his first customer ('tall Julie') and her response when she tasted a focaccia sandwich. 'That's real ham, real home cooked ham,' she said in amazement. That reaction made it worth the effort, the pride of having made someone happy with a plate of food. And the reaction from regulars has continued in that vein. The story of the Kevins is similar to that of many other people who do more than dream about opening their own place. It's a different kind of food business from the highly profitable fast food or garage forecourt trade. In a sense, the people who do it get back something of what they put in. Do it with real love and your customers will love you back. And then you're the person who created something special, a space for a group of familiar faces who are glad you're there.

The downsides? 'Working long hours, worrying about how you're going to be able to pay your bills and the stresses of working with a partner where it's easy to snap at each other.'

The payoff comes for front of house Kevin when he's standing in the place when it's all set up, everything looking great and no one there. It also happens when he stops for a moment to take it all in when the place is packed and everyone is in full flow, chatting over food they have served.

Day Thirty

I put a picture of my cupcakes on Twitter with a joke about calling them the 'bunbelievables'. It feels oddly exposed to be giving strangers something to eat that I made with my own hands, like the first time I saw my name in print in a newspaper. Of course journalists are the only people who notice bylines, their own and those of others, not the majority of readers. And fewer still people think about the producer of their morning cupcake in terms of anything other than an anonymous pair of hands.

It's St Patrick's weekend so I've mentioned them in the restaurant review page in *The Irish Times*, a fast track piece of publicity that would not be available to me if I were cooking and selling them directly in the farmers' markets.

I've printed up a laminated flyer explaining the idea behind the cupcakes and asking people to give me feedback through Twitter. 'She's a critic. She can take it,' I write, a statement at which my husband chuckles knowingly, suggesting that this is far from the truth. I'm hoping Twitter will provide a kind of virtual market, so that I can find out whether people like the cupcakes. In the end I get just one message. And Liam's right. Criticism of something you've spent long, hot hours making is not easy to take.

The Bunbelievables Recipe

(Makes between twenty and twenty four, depending on the size of your bun cases)
400g plain flour
Two tsps baking soda
One and a half tsps salt
60g pure cacao, finely grated
8 tsps sugar free cocoa powder
120g butter (melted)
120ml grape seed oil
320ml agave syrup
320ml milk
Two tsps white wine vinegar

Heat the oven to 180°C. In order put all the ingredients into a food processor and mix to a lump free batter. Line the bun tins with paper cases. Fill each one three quarters full with batter. Bake for twenty to twenty five minutes until firm. Cool on a wire tray.

Chocolate Ganache
120ml heavy cream
120ml maple syrup
100g Willie's Supreme Raw Cacao (Blue Venezuelan)
180g butter
50g hazelnuts toasted, skinned and chopped finely

Heat the cream and maple syrup in a pan. Bring it to the boil, whisking it gently. Turn off the heat and add the chopped cacao, stirring until melted. Turn off the heat. Stir in the butter one tablespoon at a time, waiting until each one is melted before adding the next. Transfer the mixture to a bowl and cool in the fridge until it has thickened to a piping consistency. Top the buns with the cooled ganache, using a palette knife or an icing bag to pipe it in a circular design. Finish with a sprinkle of chopped toasted hazelnuts.

I made too much ganache for my last batch, so had a bowl in the fridge. It makes delicious truffles, taking a teaspoonful, rolling it into a ball and dusting it with chopped nuts or cocoa powder. Alternatively just eat it straight from the bowl. The ingredients are so rich and satisfying I found it great for hitting a sweet craving square on. One small teaspoon is enough to feel like a treat and it doesn't leave you wanting more.

I come away from the experience knowing much more about how food is produced and why so much of it is so mediocre. The time and ingredients needed to produce excellent food are expensive. Most large scale food production is hard work for many people working in noisy, hot, small spaces with no natural light. It's what makes people flock to farmers' markets to taste things as they should taste: cakes made with fresh eggs rather than pasteurised bottles of goo; bread made by hand and given time to prove rather than mixed by machine and pushed by chemicals into a speedy turnaround; meat from animals reared outdoors using their muscles rather than standing in sedentary confinement packing calories away to grow from babies to heavy protein packed adults in a short few months.

All the cupcakes in Union Square are sold and all but two in Itsa, so it's been a success, albeit one with a large push from a mention in a national newspaper. Were I selling the cupcakes directly to my own customers the sixty nine cakes would have netted me a profit of roughly €100. Depending on how long it took to sell that many I could calculate the payment per hour at anywhere between €10 and €20. Factoring in the time to prepare, make, deliver and sell that number of cupcakes it would be closer to the €10 mark, barely above the minimum wage. Both shops donate all the proceeds from the buns to the charity I've nominated, the Bone Marrow for Leukaemia Trust at St James's Hospital, in memory of Maria. In Union Square they match my proceeds with the same sum from their own till.

Even with the narrower of the profit margins I have calculated I understand the attraction of making something by hand that you're proud of, using the best ingredients and giving it to people who smile and thank you. Feeding someone well means making them happy and people respond to that with great warmth and affection. But if I spent much more time working in food production I think it would blunt my ability to be critical about the end result. Even mediocre food involves hard work. It's obvious why the talented and the clever and even the not so talented or clever want to step away from the stove top and cook on camera or just talk or write about cooking. A restaurant kitchen is a physically tough workplace. A food production unit is a labour camp where no one will wonder at your prowess and the health inspector may want to see your fridge temperature chart at any given moment.

I've enjoyed the effort of pulling this last project together, although it has been a challenge to fit it into the thirty day model of going from zero to something finished. Like so much else in this year of trying, the reward has been in the doing.

8

Stepping Out of the Time Travel Machine

It became a bit of a black joke with friends: the book about using time effectively, the book that missed its own deadline. Several times. This book about roping time off and getting things done nearly didn't get written. Faced with a looming deadline and the challenge of writing I found myself failing, more badly than I had failed at anything else I tried in this busy, challenging, sad and fascinating year. Each time I sat down to concentrate something would tug my attention and I would let it drift. Many days I wouldn't even sit down, doing everything possible to avoid the desk and that lurching sensation of wondering where to start on the final chapters. I loosened the grip on my time, the boundaries I set around work and I floundered.

But I had something I didn't have before I started this project: the thirty day idea. It was an entirely artificial construct, possibly a delusional model, a gimmick, a trick. But it was the approach I eventually applied to the seventh challenge of this book: getting it written. After a particularly unproductive day I decided to sit down and write, every day for thirty days, to describe this year as honestly as I could. After ten days of writing a little every day I rediscovered the truth, variations of which I'd been discovering all year: there is no magic to getting things done, just long hours of doing it or trying to do it and ignoring the sudden compulsion to rearrange the sock drawer.

I had methods within the thirty day rule: working for a twenty or thirty minute burst, then rewarding myself with a cup of coffee, a few minutes flute playing or a skite on the Internet, before another small chunk of productivity. I rewarded myself with a break when the word count reached a certain point – gimmicky but it worked.

The looming demand of the book at the end was what got me through the point at which I wanted to stop doing each of the activities I had tried. Without the book I wouldn't have done as many things or done them so intensely within such a short space of time. But the momentum was good. By the end the whole enterprise was like a heavy iron bicycle. I had to keep moving or it would just fall over with a loud clatter.

The project was finished where it started: on our scrubbed pine kitchen table, whose surface I know intimately. I wipe it down two, maybe three times a day. There are pen marks and scratches and faded patches all over it. The varnish was wiped away progressively over the decade we've owned it. It's bleached, scrubbed, almost white in patches, dotted with brown whorls and knots like freckles on a skin. We all try to sit down around it and once a week we manage to do it without anyone shouting or having to encourage reluctant eaters. This is pizza night when Liam's home made pizza dough is topped with the things my sons like: plain ham and cheese for Shane, pineapple for his younger brothers Peter and Isaac.

Homework is done on it, board games played on it, newspapers leafed through in the calm of a quiet house in the evening. And in the end it was a clutter free calm place to finish this book, to record the final weeks of the kitchen table gap year, a year that required nothing other than some cash and a shift in mindset.

Roping off clear chunks of time to do just one thing is still something I have to remind myself to do, properly and ruthlessly, rather than half heartedly. Letting work bleed into all parts of my day makes it difficult to cope. I also have to remind myself to stop begging my children for time, asking them, 'Please give me a minute? Just one minute?' as if it's air they're taking from me in too small a space. It's not their responsibility to give me time. That's something only I can do for myself.

As they grow out of the baby stage and into boyhood I am very conscious that these are three individuals I am blessed to have a chance to share time with on this beautiful planet. It's not easy but it verges on impossible if I try to do it with one eye on a Twitter feed or an email account. Separating work from family makes time with my children much more pleasant. I don't want them to remember their parents as ghostly half presences, people who were locked in a gaze with a screen as they tugged at our sleeves for attention. And when I see them playing or talking to each other or just rapt in front of the television I want to stop the clocks and keep them like that. Mine. Here. Safe. That push me pull you of love that ebbs and flows until you're hollowed out by it. And I realise the second of those words, 'here', is the only one that is in any way true.

Children are mindful without having to try. Yes, there are the 'Are we there yet?' moments when they yearn for the next thing just as passionately as we dysfunctional adults do. But then they notice things like dust motes in sunshine. These days I try to watch them, just look at them and drink them in. I love how my eldest looks when he swims up from underwater, his thick brown hair hanging like a short curtain, then clinging like seal pelt to the curve of the back of his head. I could look at my five year old's thick, long eyelashes all day and try to fathom whether his eyes are dark green or hazel. My youngest, when he's not hurrying to be bigger, is a singer and a listener. 'Smile, Mama,' he says, with a beguiling grin, when I'm glaring at him, making it difficult to hold the glare.

I would like them to remember their mother as someone who kept on learning and trying and living, not in an embarrassing, pretend I'm still twenty fashion but in a way truer to the joy of childhood when every step is new and exciting. Learning new things has helped me to relate a bit better to the stage they are at, to tell them truthfully that difficult things get easier the more you stick at them.

They will probably inherit the love of the last minute cram, leaving things to pile up until they press you up against an immovable deadline and you have no choice but to do them. For years as a journalist, working first for a daily paper, then a weekly, I maintained that tightrope walk, pressing the send button to fire my copy into the newsdesk computer within seconds of a deadline.

I remember that feeling of reeling away from the keyboard, jittery with adrenalin and relief. It's a work regime that I loved but it probably helped lead me down the road of back trouble and anxiety, a steady, simmering presence that could have leached the joy out of life as I reached middle age and had my own mini crisis.

One of the biggest lessons of this year for me has been not the harnessing of productivity or how to motivate myself but how to rest. It happened recently in a yoga class where I found myself not just relaxing between postures but collapsing into the floor. It's taken me two years to get the hang of it, this letting go sensation, becoming as limp as a wet fish on a slab. When it happens I can feel the weight of my head, like a bowling ball. I try to imagine lying on soft sand: the cool air that comes in as the door opens is the water, gently washing over me and pushing me further into the sand underneath. Then I am taken by the pull and suck of the tide and drift out to sea. I'm as relaxed as a hank of seaweed draped and dripping over an oar. It's a profound form of rest and each time I reached it I found the next thing I had to do was slightly easier.

Real rest is difficult to come by in daily life. Plenty of friends and family have been given smartphones by their employers, work tools that they use to play with, ensuring that their link with the office is never far from hand. It's a steady bleed of work into home life and because it comes in a shiny, fun package we've welcomed it. We break away from a late night game of *Angry Birds* to respond to an angry email. And without our noticing it another bit of life has been chipped away and dropped into the maw of the ever ravenous workplace. We are selling our souls to The Man for a smartphone.

I love the Internet. I've made friends through it, found it an invaluable help in research and keeping me in touch with what's happening from the remote limb of a home office. I love that people tweet what they had for breakfast. What human activity is better than food to make you feel you know someone a bit, that you are connected to them, if only because you both love hot buttered toast or a certain brand of jam? It might be someone you've never met and will never meet but it's almost a rebellion in the virtual world to make Twitter a conversation about something as real as food.

Despite these visceral human touches the Internet is the home for that gist memory part of our brains that skims over things, the autopilot setting that we slip into so comfortably, remembering little (and yes I'm aware the Internet is full of unforgettable things) and focusing only briefly before the next bright new thing catches our attention. We are designed to interact with the physical world and many of us are spending less of our time doing that. Getting back to the physical demands of life has been an immense source of contentment for me. And trying to teach my brain to remember things again, to crank back into life as a learning machine, has been a revelation.

Away from the kitchen table I found the most productive hours of writing were spent in a plane, flying by myself on a press trip without Internet access. I had just the words of this book on my laptop screen and a babble of cheerful Danish conversation in the background. On the Faroe Islands with a group of chefs and journalists, my phone coverage died so I spent hours floating free of the online world, in a breathtaking and strange place. At one point a tall prowed red painted wooden boat came across a bay, rowed by a group of boys. Rowing is the islands' national sport and these boys were out in the sea in this remote austere place, learning and practising a physical skill that went back for generations. Something about it was profoundly moving. If I'd had a smartphone to hand no doubt I would have filmed and tweeted it. Instead I watched as they rowed from one side of the bay, a man at the front appearing to instruct and lead them. Then the boat turned and they rowed away again. I drank the sight in with my eyes: no camera, no attempt to capture it, in awe of the sheer boyness of it, the physical heft and pull in time to a rhythm and a pulse.

This simple, beautiful journey was the opposite to the ones we all make, the time travel tricks we pull on ourselves, remembering pleasure in our past and anticipating it in our future instead of finding it where we are. We spend many of our waking moments time travelling, shuttling endlessly between past and future and shouldering aside the moment we're in now in the rush to go back and forth. Losing the now. The times when we stop the time travel machine are the moments we are fully alive. Mindfulness is having its moment as people struggle with anxiety and depression. Each of the things I tried had an element of meditation: breathing, concentrating, learning, physically working in the outdoors. Each activity put me back in touch with myself.

On the press trip one of the journalists spoke about how the first thing he and his wife do after opening their eyes in the morning is to go online on their smartphones, one on each side of the bed. Often the only way of knowing if the other person has woken up first is through a Facebook update. We laughed when he told the story, with its funny, self aware and possibly exaggerated punch line.

We have given hours of our lives to the online world because it seems fun and relaxing. For me it stopped being relaxing and began to feed into that constant sense of distraction and time dribbling gist impressions. In order to make time to do the things I wanted to do for this project I stopped watching television, channel surfing and zoning out in front of 'reality' TV shows. I've never seen an episode of *X Factor* and I don't feel I've missed anything life enhancing.

I have lots of thirty day ideas I want to try in the future: relearning my basic piano skills; thirty days of kindness; thirty days of Proust or Joyce; thirty days of meditation; thirty days without sugar; thirty days to clean my house. A thirty day project is not a large amount of time but it's enough to get you started on something. If you like what you do it is enough time to turn it into a habit. It's more than four weeks, which seems blindingly obvious. But the fact that it's not measured in weeks means that you stick to counting each day rather than thinking in chunks of weeks. Taking in the weekend days as part of your regime eliminates the drag of a Monday morning, that sense of climbing back into a routine after a break.

Telling people I was doing this was also a good move. A public declaration, starting a blog, putting a calendar in the kitchen with the days marked off in large numbers, finding a thirty day buddy with whom you can do your activity – all these help to motivate when the TV remote starts to look more appealing than the drizzly evening outside.

Inadvertently this has become the opposite of a misery memoir. It's a class of contentment memoir, although not in a smug I've figured it out fashion or that threadbare idea of a 'journey' (how I hate that word with its sense of linear progression). Instead it's been about flashes of contentment, learning that happiness isn't waiting for me in a different house or a better job or better hair. It's work in progress, boosted by meeting new people and keeping in touch with old friends, by being open to new ideas and experiences and enjoying the textures of the familiar and the routine, by trying to learn and pushing myself to get better and feeling the satisfaction of something done, something achieved. The great thing about doing something intensively for thirty days, feeling pushed to the limits of time, was that stretch in the day that I got when I stopped. It was like the luxury of all that revision time after the exam was over. Soon I filled it with other things that made me feeling harried and time poor again. But for a little while it was there, my daily hour or so, that was still separate and jewel like and all mine.

I am still a procrastinator. I'm still given to moments of bleakness and heart thumping 4am jitters. I still shout at my kids more than I should. I can still be a grouchy wife. I still yearn for things I can't have. My life is far from a zen like oasis of calm. The unpainted skirting board got painted but with just one layer of undercoat.

The difference after my six months of somedays is that now I have a set of tools I can reach for when life starts to feel overwhelming. They don't come in a blister pack or a bottle and they don't require a large payment or a trip on a plane. They're all available under my roof or a short distance away. I'm a runner, a fluter, a gardener, a yoga goer, a baker and someone who can just about order a beer in Mandarin. It's been a tough and brilliant year and I take from it six lessons, which sound like cheesy T shirt slogans. But they're my cheesy T shirt slogans and I hope to be able to remember them for the rest of my days:

1. Motivation comes from doing.
2. Stay open to everything.
3. Love your mistakes and move on.
4. Mammoth becomes manageable when you do a little each day.
5. Find the lulls and luxuriate in them.
6. Just bloody do it.